Thomas E. Rogers

Records of Yarlington

Being the History of a Country Village

Thomas E. Rogers

Records of Yarlington
Being the History of a Country Village

ISBN/EAN: 9783337231323

Printed in Europe, USA, Canada, Australia, Japan

Cover: Foto ©ninafisch / pixelio.de

More available books at **www.hansebooks.com**

RECORDS OF YARLINGTON.

RECORDS OF YARLINGTON:

Being

THE HISTORY OF A COUNTRY VILLAGE.

BY

T. E. ROGERS, Esq., M.A.,

Chancellor of the Diocese of Bath and Wells, and Recorder of Wells.

LONDON:
ELLIOT STOCK, 62, PATERNOSTER ROW, E.C.
HALLETT, BATH.   JACKSON, WELLS.
BARNICOTT, TAUNTON.   SWEETMAN, WINCANTON.
1890.

To the COUNCIL AND MEMBERS

OF THE SOMERSET RECORD SOCIETY,

This Attempt

TO RESUSCITATE, FOR THE PURPOSES

OF A PARISH HISTORY,

THE DRY BONES OF SUNDRY OLD DEEDS

AND MUNIMENTS OF TITLE,

Is respectfully Inscribed;

IN THE HOPE THAT THEY WILL NOT DISDAIN

A WHOLLY UNAUTHORISED OFFERING,

WHICH THEIR OWN EXAMPLE IN SIMILAR RESEARCH

HAS SUGGESTED TO THE WRITER.

PREFACE.

'THE dullest of all dull books is a conscientiously compiled parochial history.'—*Saturday Review*, May 11th, 1889.

Undeterred, if not undismayed, by the above sweeping criticism, and without questioning the truth of it—of which, indeed, the following pages are only too likely to afford an additional illustration—the writer has nevertheless ventured to send them to the press, as containing the substance, in a somewhat expanded shape, of a lecture on 'The Records of My Village,' recently delivered by him at the neighbouring towns of Castle Cary and Wincanton.

T. E. R.

YARLINGTON HOUSE,
Michaelmas, 1889.

CONTENTS.

		PAGE
I.	THE MANOR OF YARLINGTON, FROM DOMESDAY TO 1541	1
	Pedigree of Salisbury, Plantagenet and Pole	15
II.	YARLINGTON AND ITS OWNERS FROM 1541 TO 1592: THE PARRS, SIR THOMAS SMITH, THE ROSEWELLS	20
III.	YARLINGTON AND THE BERKELEYS, FROM 1592 TO THE DEATH OF MAURICE BERKELEY, ESQ., JANUARY, 1673-74	28
	Pedigree of Berkeley, of Bruton and Yarlington	39
IV.	MADAM JAEL BERKELEY (HER TRIALS AND TRIUMPHS): THE ROYNONS AND GODOLPHINS, FROM 1673 TO 1712	45
	Pedigree of Godolphin	60
V.	THE MARQUIS OF CARMARTHEN, VENDOR, 1782	63
	APPENDIX: THE INCUMBENTS OF YARLINGTON	77
	SEPULCHRALIA	82
	INDEX	94

RECORDS OF YARLINGTON.

I.

THE MANOR OF YARLINGTON.

YARLINGTON, at the time of the Conquest, as we learn from Domesday, was known as 'Gerlingtun.' This interchange of the initial 'Y' and the hard 'G' was, as we know, and is, of very common occurrence, from the similarity of the sound in Saxon and modern German pronunciation. Yarnfield is Gernefelle, Yeovil is Givele, and the surname of Yeatman, well known in the neighbourhood, is nothing more nor less than 'Gate-man'; and their arms are charged with two gates. Yarlington was also sometimes spelt with the initial letter J — Jarlington — as 'Yatton' is Jatune; the J, of course, being pronounced as the initial Y.

But what is Gerlingtun? Is it the town of the Girlings? There is a village of Girlington in Yorkshire, and Girling survives to this day as a surname in East Anglia; and a Mrs. Girling, a woman of extraordinary force of character, was, only the other day, the life and soul of the little community of 'Shakers' who squatted in the New Forest, to the delectation and edification of the Hon. Auberon

Herbert. However this may be, and whoever gave the name to the place, such eponymous person had ceased to hold it at the time of the Conquest, when, as Domesday tells us, one Alnod held it, and was promptly dispossessed by the Conqueror; and the Manor, with many others in the county, was conferred on his half-brother, Robert, Earl of Morton, or Mortain, in Normandy. The Domesday account is:

'The Earl himself holds Gerlingtun. Alnod held it T.R.E., and gelded for 7 hides. The land is 7 carucæ. In demesne is 1 caruca and 6 serfs, and 8 villeins and 6 bordarii, with 2 carucæ. There is a mill which is worth 7s. rent, a wood 6 quarentines long and 3 broad. It was worth £7, is now worth 100s.'

These dimensions are reduced by the learned Mr. Eyton ('Somerset,' vol. i., p. 118) as follows: '7 quasi-hides, plough-lands, 840 acres; wood, 180 acres. Total measurement, 1,020 acres.'

The Manor passed from this powerful Earl Robert to his son William, who was, however, deprived of all his estates by his cousin, Henry I., in consequence of his siding with Robert Curthose, Duke of Normandy, in the contentions between him and Henry; and all the Morton estates in Somerset were then granted by the King to the baronial family of Montacute, which was now attaining to great power. Its ancestor, Drogo of Montacute, was the confidential friend and comrade-in-arms of Robert, Earl of Morton, and already possessed many manors under him as his feudal lord, as Shepton Montague, Sutton Montis, Donyatt, a hide of land in Montacute, etc., and the Barons of Montacute now fairly step into the shoes of the Earls of Morton. The second Earl of Morton had, however, parted with many of his Manors before the confiscation of his estates, and amongst the estates so parted with was that of the Castle of Montacute and Manor of 'Bishopstone,' by which latter name the parish of Montacute was then known.

'The Earl himself' (says Domesday) 'had in demesne Bishopstone, and there is his castle, which is called Montagud.' This manor and castle had been granted by William, second Earl of Morton, to a priory of Cluniac monks which he there established. Amongst the estates thus made over to the priory, Collinson (vol. iii., p. 312) enumerates 'the church of Yarlington.' The Montacutes must, however, in some way have recovered the advowson. In the earliest register existing at Wells, Bishop Drokensford's (*temp.* Edward II.), so admirably edited for the Somerset Record Society by my old playmate ('for we were nursed upon the self-same hill') and college contemporary, Bishop Hobhouse, the presentations to the living are duly entered as by the Montacutes;[1] and in 1315 one William (de Glideford), Rector of Yarlington, and Sir Simon de Montacute, are commissioned by Bishop Drokensford to take charge of the goods and persons of the nuns of Whitehall, Ilchester, and to deliver to him an account of their administration. In the 'Valor' of 1290 the Prior of Montacute received a yearly pension of 10s. out of the Rectory; but the advowson at that time was not in the Priory, which looks as if some compromise had been made

---

[1] And see Weaver's 'Somerset Incumbents:' Yarlington.

between the Montacutes and the Priors. In the 'Valor' of Henry VIII. the pension no longer appears. It may have been redeemed, or have been only payable for so many lives or years.

It is abundantly clear that the Montacutes did not take their designation from the parish of Montacute, where, in the time of Robert, Earl of Morton, they only held a hide of land under him as their feudal lord. Shepton Montague, the neighbouring village to Yarlington, appears to have been the 'caput baroniæ,' although there is no evidence of any capital mansion there; and Sutton Montis also takes its second name from them.

The Manor of Yarlington was held by this powerful family, Barons of Montacute, and afterwards Earls of Salisbury, for nearly 450 years, viz., from the end of the eleventh century (1091) to 1339, when, upon the attainder of Margaret, Countess of Salisbury, following upon that in 1521 of her son-in-law, Edward, Duke of Buckingham, the Manor finally reverted to the Crown.

There is no place known in the county of Somerset of sufficient size or importance to have formed the principal country-seat of this great and powerful family. There was a mansion and park at Donyatt (the park is noticed in Domesday, 'ibi-parcus'), and the mansion there was fortified (2 Edward III.) by William of Montacute, first Earl of Salisbury. It seems probable that, being constantly employed in the service of the Crown, they had, when not engaged in the King's wars, their chief quarters in London, and only paid occasional visits to their various country seats in the West of England. Their Manor-house at Yarlington, from its situation, could scarcely have had capacity for the retinue of a powerful Norman nobleman. King John, however, as appears from his 'Itinerary,' slept there for a night or two when on one of his hunting expeditions, as lying between the Blackmoor Vale Forest and Selwood Forest, where he had a hunting-box at Brewham Lodge; and Simon, sixth Baron Montacute, who appears to have been much at Yarlington, obtained in 1313 (7 Edward II.) license to fortify his Manor-house here; and in the Cal^m Rot^m Chartarum (p. 147), Edward II., No. 8, Chart. 47, is a charter to this Simon de Montacute of a fair, 'mercata feria,' at Yarlington, and also at Chedzoy; and right of free warren to these two Manors, and also to Thurlbear, Shepton Montague, and Donyatt.

The fortification at Yarlington consisted of a moat on the east and south sides of the church and Manor-house, which is still plainly visible, and which, being cut through higher ground in a loop or half-circle from a lake of some fourteen acres, which extended along the low ground on the north and west sides of the church and Manor-house, placed them in a small island, completely detached from the rest of the village, from which the access was by a drawbridge over the moat, where the road by the present blacksmith's shop leads to the church. Where this moat again joined the lake, on the west side of the bridge, was 'the pond-head'; and here, in after-days (1562), a mill was built, with a good fall from the water of the stream, which was here bayed back to form the lake. The island was itself so small that the Manor-house could at no time have been very large. But all the offices, stables, and the like, were on the other side of the water, where the farmhouse now stands. This is shown by the names of the fields—Court Field, Pigeon-house Field, and (of course, much later on), Potatoe Sleight. In 1875, when the old farmhouse, which had been burned down, was being rebuilt, the contractor, knowing nothing of its history, came to inform me that, to his surprise, there were evident remains of a stable in the old house. There was also a very extensive deer-park on the whole of the north and east sides of the Manor, and fields bear the names of Buck Park and Hind Park, which latter, however, has lost its name and place within my memory, having been thrown into a larger field of a different name.

In connection with this park there was a very unusual right claimed by the Lords of the Manor; that of 'the Deer's Leap,' as it was locally called, and which was a claim to all timber growing within six feet, not from the stem of the hedge, but from the sheer of the outside ditch, and in certain parts, adjoining Bratton and Maperton, within fifteen and a half feet;[1] and in the various perambulations of the Manor the timber-trees so growing are duly enumerated and particularised as belonging to the Lords of the Manor of Yarlington; and in the old parish maps

---

[1] *E.g.* 'From Whatley Ball—where the park wall formerly stood—the Lord of this Manor' (Yarlington) 'claims 15½ feet.'—Perambulations, 1754, 1783. The Court Rolls in my possession do not reach back beyond 1746. The custom of the Manor was that 'at the Court Leet and Court Baron of the Lord,' holden annually in the third week of October, a tenant was admitted for three lives, with a Heriot or Fine upon each life succeeding as tenant, with benefit of widowhood to the widow of the last surviving life. It was in this 'widow's estate' that the customary tenant of the Manor chiefly differed from the ordinary freehold leaseholder; except, indeed, that by the mode of assurance he enjoyed practical immunity as well from the imposition of the Stamp Duty as from 'the tyranny of parchment.'

a dotted line outside the parish boundaries is marked round that part of the parish to which this right was alleged to attach; commencing from 'the Slait Gate' at the bottom of 'Great Slait,' and going round by Hadspen, Bratton, and Clapton in Maperton, to a spot since known as Amen Corner, where Yarlington Manor, Woolston in the parish of Yarlington, and Clapton in the parish of Maperton, conjoin. Thus, in 1754, in the 'Record of a Perambulation,' stated in the caption to be 'in and for the Manor of Yarlington, then in the possession of Francis, Earl of Godolphin, for settling the bounds and privileges of such Manor, due notice being timely given to the respective proprietors of lands and Manors adjoining,' the account goes on to say: 'We set out from Slait Gate; from thence the procession runs six feet on the level round the outside of the fence bordering on Vickris Dickinson, Esq.,[1] in whose first field, called "Harewells," were three oaks and one elm, adjudged to belong to the said Earl of Godolphin;' and so on as regards specified trees, at six feet and fifteen and a half feet respectively, in the adjoining lands of Hadspen, and of Bratton, and Clapton in Maperton, and signed:

   'RICHARD GAPPER, Rector,
   GEO. BOWYER, Curate,
   JNO. YEATMAN, Deputy Steward,
   MAURICE CORNISH, Churchwarden,'

and by many other names still known in the parish; *e.g.*, Josiah White, James Davidge, Wm. Day, Isaac Garland, Thos. Bishop, Walter Hix, etc.

---

[1] The then owner of the Hadspen Estate.

This may be a fitting place to note once for all the peculiar position which Woolston Farm, or Woolston Manor Farm, holds in regard to Yarlington.[1] At no time does this compact little estate of 230 acres, lying on the south of the parish, appear to have been comprehended under the title of 'the Manor of Yarlington,' if, indeed, it ever formed part of the Montacute property. Indeed, it seems doubtful whether it is included in Domesday—at least, under the head of Yarlington. Mr. Eyton, as we have seen, reduces the Domesday quantities to 1,020, which is within forty acres of the actual extent of the parish, exclusive of Woolston Farm. The acreage, however, as given in Domesday, of both Blackford and Maperton parishes, which also abut on Woolston Farm, are largely in excess of their modern acreage; Blackford being stated at 1,045, as against its modern acreage of 578 acres; and Maperton at 1,715, against 1,534 acres; so that Woolston Farm may have inadvertently got included in one of these parishes.

On the other hand, in the oldest description I have of it, at the beginning of the seventeenth century, the estate is designated as 'Great Woolston, otherwise Woolston Gyon;' and in the Kirkby Quest, *temp.* Edward III., two persons of the name of Gyon are entered as in Yarlington parish,[2] who were, no doubt, the eponymous owners of this farm.

---

[1] Woolston *proper*, if I may so call it—that is, Woolston as distinct from Woolston Farm—is a populous and considerable hamlet, wholly comprised in the parish of North Cadbury.

[2] I am indebted for this information to the kindness of my neighbour, Mr. Dickinson, of Kingweston, whose promised publication of 'Kirkby's Quest' is expected with interest by his friends of the Somerset Record Society.

Again, following up this clue, it is noteworthy that when Dru, or Drogo, de Montacute certified the smaller knights' fees of his barony, for the purposes of assessment on the marriage of the daughter of Henry II., he returns, with nine others, a certain John (or Jordan) *Guihane* for one knight's fee. (Collinson, iii. 46.) Now, this Guihane looks' or, at any rate, sounds, very like an earlier form of Gyon; and this knight's fee may very probably be in respect of Woolston in Yarlington, which was then, or afterwards, dissevered from the barony. Very early in the seventeenth century the estate was owned by the Chafins, or Chafyns, of Chettle and of Folke in Dorset, a family of large possessions in Dorset, Somerset, and Wilts, and now represented by Miss Chafyn Grove, of Zeals.[1] It was purchased from the Chafins in the middle of the last century, by a Mr. James Harding, of Mere, merchant, whose family held it for two or three generations, and some of whom resided there, as yeomen, in the first quarter of the present century.

To return to the old claim of 'the Deer's Leap,' and the timber thereon. It formed, more than eighty years ago, the subject of a characteristic correspondence between my grandfather, the then owner of the Manor, and two neighbouring squires. My ancestor, desiring to remove what might prove a source of litigation or dispute in the future, addressed himself to Mr. Hobhouse and to Colonel Pen-

---

[1] The Chafins were Sheriffs of Dorset, *temp*. Elizabeth, and Bamfield Chafin was Sheriff of the same county in 1624. In 1634, through the concession of Sir Henry Berkeley, he presented to the living of Yarlington.

ruddock, the owner of Clapton, with a view to an amicable adjustment and settlement of all claims. The following is a copy of Mr. Hobhouse's answer, the original of which is now in my possession :

'HADSPEN,
'*Oct.* 20*th*, 1807.

'DEAR SIR,

'I have received your letter of yesterday respecting a claim which you state the proprietor of the Manor of Yarlington to have upon some timber growing within certain limits of its border adjoining to Hadspen, and with which you conceive me to be well acquainted.

'With the existence of such a claim I am certainly not wholly unacquainted, because you once hinted at it in a conversation with me several years ago, but of its foundation or its extent I am completely uninformed. And, to say the truth, as I have never since heard of it again, I concluded you had abandoned it as untenable. It struck me when you first alluded to it as a claim so very extraordinary, that I took some pains to see whether I could find any vestige of it in any documents in my possession. But so far have I been from tracing it, that, on the contrary, I find my land has been uniformly conveyed from seller to buyer, *together with all timber and other trees growing* thereon. Nor have I been able to learn that the claim has ever been either exercised by the owner of Yarlington, or recognised by the owner of Hadspen.

'You do me but justice in supposing that I shall be inclined to settle the matter amicably. No one can be more strongly disposed than I am to avoid disputes with my neighbours, and I trust that none will arise out of the present question. But, in the absence of all information on the subject, you will excuse me for saying that *at present* I see nothing to ask any common friend to decide on. If you will have the goodness to point out to me how your claim originated, or in what manner or at what period the supposed right has either been exercised by the owner of your estate or admitted by the owner of mine, it may lay the foundation of an enquiry more successful than I have hitherto instituted, or of a different determination from any I can form in my present state of darkness.

'As my stay at this place is unfortunately limited to the present week, you will do me a favour by enabling me by an early answer to make such an enquiry within that period.

'I am, dear Sir,
'Yours most faithfully,
'H. HOBHOUSE.'

A negotiation entered upon in such a spirit on both sides could not fail of a satisfactory result. My ancestor set no value on his claim, and only wished to secure his descendants from any temptation to embark on any litigation in the assertion of it. It was therefore agreed that, in consideration of my grandfather's cutting down a tree, he should release all claim, Mr. Hobhouse sagely suggesting that, as it purported to be a release of right in realty, it ought to be under seal, and that he would therefore prepare a short deed for my grandfather's signature, which no doubt is to this day in the Hadspen archives.[1] My ancestor's

---

[1] It would ill accord with my feelings as a man, not to say a Somersetshire man, if I were to pass over the name of the Right Hon. Henry Hobhouse without some notice of this late eminent owner of Hadspen. An elegant scholar (as is evidenced by his Greek translation in the 'Musæ Etonenses' of Milton's 'Invocation to Light'), a most accurate and profound lawyer, whose opinion, whether as chamber counsel, or as legal adviser to the Treasury and Home Office, was regarded as second to none of the Judges on the Bench, a diligent and painstaking investigator and collector of all records and facts bearing upon the history of the county, a well-informed and conscientious Churchman, he was, perhaps, nowhere seen to greater advantage than as a resident country gentleman, a magistrate of the county, and chairman of Quarter Sessions. Whilst in the successive offices of State which he filled, he so recommended himself to the highest authorities, that he was selected as one of the executors of his will by Sir Robert Peel, whom he survived, although the Prime Minister was by many years his junior. To his kindly precepts and advice, readily given at all times, no less than to his powerful example, as landlord, neighbour, and friend, I have ever felt and acknowledged that I owe my early aspirations to employ whatever small abilities I might possess in the immediate sphere of my own people, amongst whom I was born ; and thus to utilise and illustrate to the best of my power the rather limited and narrow conditions of the line of life—the 'fallentis semita vitæ'—which it is the lot of the country gentleman to pursue In the course of a long life, and whilst in chambers at Lincoln's Inn, I have,

application to Colonel Penruddock met with a more militant response. 'If the Lord of the Manor of Yarlington thinks that he has any claim to timber growing on my estate at Clapton, he had better take steps to enforce such claim.'

Here the matter ended; but in the next Perambulation entered on the Court Rolls, in 1811, the old specification of the timber trees outside the boundary of the Manor is discontinued; and, indeed, for all practical purposes, the only usage in later times had consisted in the custom of keeping outside the boundary-fence for shooting or coursing purposes, without feeling the guilty consciousness of committing a trespass. Although, indeed, upon reflection, it seems more than doubtful whether this practice could have been justified as within the alleged claim, which appears not to have extended to a general right over the land, but to have been limited to a right to the timber growing within the prescribed area. Such a claim as this, to timber on another man's land, was of course in violent antagonism to common law, but it affords evidence of the pretensions of these old Norman barons.

To continue the history of the Manor. The grandson of Simon, sixth Baron of Montacute, was William, eighth Baron, who had license to fortify his mansion at Donyatt,

---

had the good fortune to be thrown into terms of intimate acquaintance and friendship with Lord Chancellors and others who have achieved the highest position in Church and State (including, indeed, two of his own distinguished sons, Bishop Hobhouse and Lord Hobhouse), yet I desire to place on record that the matured convictions and experience of my manhood only tended to sustain and confirm my youthful impressions; and that I never met with anyone who so completely realized my ideal of 'the great and good man,' the 'vir pietate gravis'—'justissimus unus qui fuit'—a tower of strength in himself, four-square against all surrounding circumstances, as did the late Right Hon. Henry Hobhouse. 'Ex abundantiâ cordis os loquitur.'

where, as we have seen, he had a park, mentioned in Domesday. He was created first Earl of Salisbury (10 Edward III., 1336-37). His son William, second Earl of Salisbury, married Elizabeth, daughter of John, Lord Mohun of Dunster, and it was in honour of this fair lady that the too susceptible King is said to have founded his Order of the Garter, in 1349. Her sister, Philippa, married, as her third husband, Edmund Plantagenet, Duke of York, the King's third son. Her second husband, Sir R. Golofre, was called Lord of Langley; and it would seem that, by reason of his marriage with her, Edmund Plantagenet assumed the surname of De Langley. (See Sir H. Nicolas, 'Historic Peerage,' note at p. 324, under 'Mohun of Dunster.')

Thomas, the fourth Earl of Salisbury, and ninth Baron Montacute, married Alice, daughter and heiress of Thomas Chaucer, and grand-daughter of the poet Chaucer. The Earl was killed at Orleans, in 1428, and their sole child and heiress, Alice, carried the property of Salisbury and the Montacutes into the house of Neville, by her marriage with Richard Neville (afterwards created Earl of Salisbury), third son of Ralph Neville, first Earl of Westmoreland. Their eldest son was Richard, the great Earl of Warwick, 'the King-maker,' and it is generally considered that the old church at Yarlington was built by him. The architec ture was of his period, and there was (as noticed by Phelps) a rose—the well-known cognizance of York and Lancaster —sculptured on one of the outside walls. The church itself, having fallen into decay, was, with the exception of the chancel and the tower, entirely rebuilt and enlarged in 1878, at a cost of over £2,000; three-fourths of the expense having been contributed by the liberality of the present Rector, the Rev. A. J. Rogers, who is also patron of the living. The sculptured rose, having become derelict, has now found a place in some rockwork in my garden.

'The King-maker's' two daughters and co-heiresses, the Lady Isabel and the Lady Anne Neville, of whom the first married George, Duke of Clarence, and the latter Richard of Gloucester, died—the Lady Isabel in 1476, and the Lady Anne in 1488. The only son of the Lady Isabel, the unfortunate young Earl of Warwick, would then, in the natural course of events, have succeeded to the enjoyment of the Montacute and Salisbury estates, but the jealousy of his uncle Richard, and, still more, the gloomy suspicions of Richmond, doomed this last of the male line of the Plantagenets to close and life-long custody until his execution, in 1499.

In 1463, the year before his death, 'the King-maker' had presented, as patron, to the Rectory of Yarlington; but in 1493, and again in 1497, 'Henricus VII. Rex' exercised this right; he being, in a very strict sense, the custos or guardian of his imprisoned victim. On Warwick's death, in 1499, his sister Margaret, Countess of Salisbury, and wife of Sir Richard Pole, became entitled to the Manor, and held it until her attainder in 1539, followed by her execution in 1541, when it finally devolved on the Crown. Collinson says it passed through the Poles to the Duke of Buckingham. Phelps, whose whole account of this parish, from beginning to end, is a tissue of small inaccuracies, says, from 'Magna Britannia,' that Margaret, Countess of

PEDIGREE OF SALISBURY, PLANTAGENET AND POLE.

```
ALICE,=THOMAS, 4th Earl of Salisbury, Baron Montacute and Monthermer
née Chaucer, widow |        killed at Orleans, 1428.
of Sir John Philips,|
m. as 3rd husb. Wm. |
De la Pole, Duke of |
Suffolk.            |
                    |
        ALICE,=Richard Neville, Earl of Salisbury, 3rd son of Ralph,
        Sole heiress. |   1st Earl of Westmoreland, beheaded at Pomfret,
                      |   1460.
            _____|_____
            |                                   |
Ann de Beauchamp,=RICHARD NEVILLE              JOHN NEVILLE,
sister and heiress |  ('King-maker'),          Marquis of Montague, killed at Barnet, 1471.
of the Duke of     |  Earl of Warwick, killed
Warwick.           |  at Barnet, 1471.
        _____|_____
        |                                                 |
George,=ISABEL, d. 1476,                    Edward,=(1) ANNE=(2) Richard, Duke of Gloucester,
Duke of  daughter and co-heiress.           Prince of   d. & co-    1472-73.
Clarence.                                   Wales,      heiress,
        |                                   son of      d. 1485.
        |                                   Henry VI,
        |                                   killed at
        |                                   Tewkes-
        |                                   bury, 1471.
  _____|_____
  |                                 |
EDWARD, Earl of Warwick,    MARGARET,=Sir Richard Pole.         Edward Plantagenet, cr. Earl of
beheaded, 1499.             Countess of Salis-                  Salisbury, d. 1484, æt. 10.
                            bury, attainted,                        |
                            1539; beheaded,                     Henry Stafford, Duke of
                            1541.                               Buckingham, be-
                                |                               headed, 1483.
       _____|_____
       |                         |                     |                |
Henry Pole, Lord Montague,  Reginald, Cardinal Pole.  URSULA=Edward Stafford, Duke of
attainted and beheaded,                                      Buckingham, attainted
1539.                                                        and beheaded, 1521.
   |
Winifred=Sir Thos. Hastings, brother of
 d. & co-    2nd Earl of Huntingdon.
 heiress.
   |
Francis,=Katharine, d. & co-heiress.
2nd Earl of
Huntingdon.
```

Salisbury, settled this Manor, with others, by a covenant with the Duke of Buckingham, in order to a marriage of her daughter Ursula with the Duke's son. But all this is not very intelligible. Henry Stafford, second Duke of Buckingham, who succeeded his grandfather, the first Duke, was beheaded and attainted in 1483, at the early age of twenty-eight, and before the Countess of Salisbury became possessed of the Manor. Edward, his son, the third and last Duke, was restored in 1486, then a minor; and it is possible that, on her daughter Ursula's marriage with this Duke Edward, the Countess may have settled the reversion on them, subject to her own life; or, again, she may have entailed it at once on them, reserving the reversion to herself. In either case the attainder and execution of the Duke, in 1521, would place her in possession of her former estate, which would thus pass altogether to the Crown on her own attainder, in 1539. As will hereafter appear, the estate was regarded by the Crown as that of the Countess, and not of the Buckinghams, and the two salient facts are these: (1) that the old Countess of Salisbury was barbarously executed in 1541, and (2) that in 1543-44—two years after—we find Henry VIII. dealing with the Manor.

But it is time to turn from the devolution of the Manor to consider what may be said as to the internal condition of the parish itself. A parish without a history may be assumed to be a happy parish, and there seems evidence of this parish leading the ordinary parochial life.

There is a field called 'Revelands,' with a fine slope to the south, where of course the usual wakes and revels were duly held. There is, as in so many other villages, a considerable tract of land called 'Breach-lands,' a name not yet explained that I am aware of;[1] but a portion of this tract consists of a field of some twelve acres, which holds on the parish map the double names of 'Parish Breach' and 'Lottsome.' This is evidently where the parish allotments were formerly established. It is unquestionably the poorest field in the parish, but whether this was the reason, or is the result, of its public user, it may be difficult to say. The greater part of the high table-land, commencing on the north-west side of the main road, opposite the roadside pump, and stretching on past the present mansion-house, was open down, or common land, of some fifty acres, upon which, as appears from the Court Rolls, the farm tenants of the Manor had common, without stint, from Candlemas to Michaelmas—from Michaelmas to St. Thomas's Day, no tenant to stock more than three sheep to an acre, and no to be folded off; and from St. Thomas to Candlemas to be 'hayned,' or shut off.

For the rest, the little parish has always been as self-sufficing and self-contained as any village of its size, with a population of about 220, and an area of some 1,200 acres, can well be. Besides corn-farmers and dairy-farmers and farm-labourers, it can boast of its own innkeeper, miller, baker, blacksmith, carpenter, mason, thatcher, sawyer, and road contractor—which is what few other small village communities can say.

To Dryasdust's scornful inquiry for antiquities, answer can only be made with 'bated breath.' But on the north

---

[1] An obvious analogy, indeed, suggests 'Breach' as a form of 'brecc,' 'brake,' and so 'Breach-land' as 'Brake-land.'

and north-west of the parish there are well-defined earthworks or escarpments (locally termed 'lynchets'), which were probably outposts of the great central stronghold of Cadbury Camp.

We have also, set up on the brow of a steep eminence, in a wood called Seamark, a large stone, or monolith, apparently of forest marble, known to the natives as Seamark Stone;[1] where some British chief may have summoned his followers to lay down the law, or some heathen priest may have offered his sacrifices. Who knows?

A stone coffin of large dimensions was found under the chancel floor in 1878, of Hamhill stone, six feet in length, twenty inches across the shoulder, fifteen inches at foot, ten inches in depth, with two round holes, one inch in diameter, drilled in the bottom, at about the small of the back. There was a thin, flat covering-stone over it, which was shivered when the coffin was disinterred. It contained a Hamhill-stone ornament in shape like a figure 8, but with the much larger or bottom circle solid—or, rather, like a large earring or a pilgrim's bottle—in dimension, one and three-quarter inches in length, and one inch in breadth. This has been shown to many antiquaries, in the hope that it might denote the age of the coffin, but at present no one has been able to make anything of it, or explain its use. There were no human remains in the coffin, which must, without doubt, have been previously disturbed and reinterred on the entire rebuilding of the chancel by Canon Frankland, in 1822. At first it seemed to me possible that

---

[1] Seamark being the name as well of some adjoining fields as of the wood itself.

the coffin might be that of Simon de Montacute; but that most careful antiquary, Bishop Hobhouse, informs me that this is not very probable, since the Montacutes, as a rule, claimed burial at Bruton Priory -- of which they were regarded as part-founders and as benefactors, and as entitled to the benefit of intercessory prayers, in consideration of their donation of the great tithes of Shepton Montague.

No natural curiosities? Well, yes; we have a hole, swallet, or chasm, into which a winter brook discharges itself, and no mortal can say where the water again issues forth.

II.

YARLINGTON AND ITS OWNERS
FROM 1541 TO 1592.

THE PARRS, SIR THOMAS SMITH, THE ROSEWELLS.

To resume our narrative. It has been mentioned that Margaret, Countess of Salisbury, was executed in 1541, and that Henry VIII. proceeded to deal with the forfeited Manor about two years after this; and from henceforth the history of the Manor has been entirely made out by myself, by the aid of old title-deeds and documents in my possession.

On 25th February, 1543-44 (anno regni 35), Henry VIII. granted this Manor and the fairs and markets there, on the nativity of our blessed Ladye the Virgin, to Queen Katharine Parr for her life, as part of her dower. On 20th August, 1547 (1 Edward VI.), the reversion in fee of the Manor and advowson (*i.e.*, subject to the Queen-Dowager's life) was granted under the great seal to her brother William, Lord Parr, Marquis of Northampton, subject to an annuity of £3 3s. 5½d., payable to the Court of Augmentations. Possibly this amount was fixed as being a tenth of the annual value of the property. In the same year (20th October, 1547) the Marquis of Northampton obtained license to alien, and on the 14th November of the same year did alien, his reversion to Thomas Smith, Esq., D.C.L., for £285 8s. 9d. The seal to this conveyance is in the most perfect state of preservation. It gives the arms of Lord Parr, surrounded by the Order of the Garter. 'Sigillum Will-mi Comitis Essex Dni Parre Dni Marmion & Scti Quintin et de Kendal.' The seal had not been renewed to add the title of Marquis de Northampton, which he had been created the previous February (1 Edward VI.), and by which title he is duly described in the deed itself.

This Thomas Smith, or Smyth (for his name is indifferently spelt both ways, and in the deed of conveyance to him is spelt both Smyth and Smythe), born in 1512, was knighted in 1548, the year after his purchase of Yarlington. He was a man of great learning and experience in State affairs. Before attaching himself to the interests of the Protector Somerset, whose secretary he was, he had been, in 1531, Fellow of Queen's College, Cambridge, and gave Greek lectures there, in which language he was a great proficient. In 1536 (being twenty-four years old), he was University Orator; in 1542, D.C.L. and Regius Professor of Civil Law. He was employed in 1548 as Ambassador at Brussels, and in 1551 as Ambassador to France. While in France he wrote in Latin and English his work on 'The Commonwealth of England,' a book still to be seen sometimes on old bookstalls. It was not published, however, till after his death, which happened in 1577. Wood says he was Provost of Eton, but was dismissed by Queen Mary with a pension of £100 a year. He adds that he was a native of Essex, and was, with his wife, buried at

Theydon Mount, in that county. Strype, who published in 1698 a 'Life' of Smith, says that 'he purchased for £300 the Manor of Yarlington, worth £30 a year, from the Marquis of Northampton, with monies he had gotten at Cambridge before he entered the Lord Protector's service.' But this usually accurate writer, when suggesting that Smith was getting ten per cent. on his purchase-money, ignores the fact that it was a reversion that he had bought. It was, however, a fortunate purchase for Smith, as the reversion fell into possession by the death of Queen Katharine in the following year. There must have been an absence of refinement, not to say a positively coarse fibre, in this Queen's constitution, which, however, does not appear to stand in the way of her being a general favourite with the writers of her time. Hume, in his dispassionate way, contents himself with describing her as 'a woman of virtue, and somewhat inclined to the new doctrine.' Born in or about 1510, she had married, first, Edward Burgh, and, secondly, John Neville, Lord Latimer; Lord Latimer having died in 1542, she was married to Henry VIII., as her third husband, in July, 1543; and the breath was scarcely out of the King's body when, to quote Hume once more, 'forgetting her usual prudence and delicacy,' she again married, as her fourth husband, the Lord High Admiral, Lord Seymour, of Sudeley, the violent and turbulent younger brother of the Protector Somerset, and died in childbed, her last moments being embittered, if not actually hastened, by the knowledge that her ill-conditioned lord was already actively engaged in transferring his attentions and caresses upon her step-daughter, the Princess

Elizabeth, a young lady who had herself inherited from both her parents a palpable strain of indelicacy and a lamentable pruriency of imagination, which were constantly in evidence all through her life, to the disfigurement of her other great qualities.

Our narrative gladly turns from these two royal favourers 'of the new doctrine' to say a word in behalf of another Queen of a very different cast of character, and who probably has been more rancorously and persistently maligned by history than any one of our sovereigns. I refer to Mary Tudor. In 1520, when she was five years old, Bishop Fox[1] could write to the King her father, then in France, that he and the Duke of Norfolk 'were on Saturday last at Richmond with the Princess Mary, who, lauded be Almighty God! is right merry and in prosperous health and state, daily exercising herself in virtuous pastimes.' But seven years after this, when she was twelve years old, the Divorce question began to agitate the royal breast, and thenceforth nothing but contradictions, vexations, and disappointments fell to the lot of this sorely-tried Princess. The cruel treatment of her gentle-natured mother filled her with a dutiful resentment against those whose tenets she not unreasonably regarded as responsible for such treatment; while, as concerned herself, she found herself suddenly and shamefully degraded from the position of Princess Royal of England to that of an illegitimate daughter of the King. A serious and settled gloom thenceforward took

---

[1] Quoted in a very full life of this prelate, prefixed to his register as Bishop of Bath and Wells, recently edited with great care by another old school and form fellow of mine, Mr. Chisholm Batten, of Thorn Falcon.

the place of her natural gaiety of heart, yet her conduct at all times appears to have been dictated simply by a sense of religious duty, and by a desire to redress some of the many acts of wrongful violence which had been committed by her royal father, without the imputation of any personal considerations or the admixture of private or revengeful feelings; and her character is now receiving more and more favourable lights, thrown upon it by every fresh State document or record which modern research brings to our notice.[1]

It has been stated that Henry VIII. confiscated all the Salisbury property on the attainder and execution of the old Countess of Salisbury, the King's first cousin once removed. At the accession of Mary the heirs of the Countess were her two granddaughters, daughters of Henry Pole, Lord Montague, viz., Katharine, wife of Francis, Earl of Huntingdon, and Winifred, wife of Sir Thomas Hastings, brother of the Earl of Huntingdon;[2] and, in the first year of Queen Mary, the castles, manors, lordships, and lands therein specified were granted by letters patent from the Queen to Francis, Earl of Huntingdon, and Katharine his wife ('our cousin' and heir of Margaret, Countess of Salisbury), and the heirs of her body, with remainder to Winifred, wife of Sir Thomas Hastings, Knight (another such cousin and heir), and the heirs of her body, remainder to the heirs of the body of the

---

[1] The depth and warmth of Mary's feelings are shown, as a daughter, in her devotion to her discarded mother; as a wife, in her touching affection for her unsympathetic consort; and as a queen, by her heart-searching distress that her reign should be signalized by the loss to the nation of Calais.

[2] See pedigree, *supra*, p. 15.

Countess, to be held of the Queen as they were held of Henry VIII. *at the attainder of the said Countess.*

The Manor of Yarlington, having been already granted by the Crown, was not, of course, included in this grant, but the grant carried the fee-farm rent of £3 3s. 5½d., which had been reserved by 1 Edward VI.

In 1555 Sir Thomas Smith presented one Roger Boydell to the living, and the year following, under the description of 'Sir Thomas Smith, of Ankerwicke, in the county of Berks, Knight,' he, by deed of 6th July, 1556, sold the Manor and advowson to William Rosewell, of Loxton, in the county of Somerset, gentleman, and William Rosewell, his son and heir apparent, 'of the Middle Temple, in the suburbs of the Citie of London,' for £1,000, whereof £100 is paid down, and the remaining £900 to be paid 'on the Feaste of Seinte Michael Th'archangel, at the house of Sir Thos. Smith's brother, George Smith, in the parishe of St. Margarette, in Lothbury.' Sir Thomas covenants that Dame Philippa, his wife, shall release dower; and by deed of 4th November, 1556, reciting that the money had been duly paid, the release to the Rosewells is executed accordingly.

This William Rosewell, the son, a barrister of the Middle Temple, came to reside at the Manor-house (presumably during the long vacations), for by a lease, *dated* 1562, in which he is described as 'Solicitor-General to our Sovereign Lady the Queen's Majesty,' the two Rosewells, father and son, demise to Richard Fitzjames, of Woolston, and Mary his wife, the capital messuage and farm of Yarlington, *late in the occupation of William Rosewell the son*, for ninety-nine years, if Fitzjames and his wife, and their son, John Fitzjames, should so long live. The premium paid down was £360, and a yearly rent of £14 12s. 8d., and the best beast as a heriot. The Solicitor-General died in the lifetime of his father, and by a deed, dated 18th April, 1569, reciting this fact, the Fitzjameses, in consideration of a payment of £700, reassign the estate for years to the elder Rosewell, still described as of Loxton, gentleman. It is clear from the difference in the two sums, £360 and £700, after an interval of only seven years, that Fitzjames had been an improving lessee; and it is mentioned in the lease of 1562, that 'Fitzjames was minded to build a Mill at the Pond-Head,' which accounts for the increased value of the premises. In the meantime the Solicitor-General, who had evidently prospered in his profession, had purchased, on his own account, Forde Abbey, in Devonshire, from the Sir Amias Paulet who had charge of the unfortunate Queen of Scots. In 1573, April 11th, a William Rosewell is presented to the Rectory of Yarlington, by Wm. Rosewell, of Loxton, gentleman. This presentee was apparently a nephew of the Solicitor-General, and a son of Thomas Rosewell, of Dunkerton, who is concerned in the presentation, and the living was held by him until 1627.

And in 1592, the Rosewells having held the Manor for thirty-six years, and the death of the father having followed that of the Solicitor-General, the William Rosewell of the third generation, the son of the Solicitor-General, and who is described in the deed of conveyance as 'William Rosewell, of Forde, in the county of Devon, esquire,'[1] sells the

---

[1] Sir Henry Rosewell, of Ford Abbey, was Sheriff of Devon in 1628; and in 1649 Ford passed from him by sale to Edmund Prideaux. Mr. Pulman in his

Manor and advowson of Yarlington to Sir Henry Berkeley, of Bruton. The conveyance was dated 8th February, 1592, and the purchase-money was £2,400, and William Rosewell's wife, 'Anne,' is to join in a fine.

Before parting company with the Rosewells, it is perhaps only fair to them to say that the rose sculptured in the church may possibly be their rebus, in allusion to their surname; but this is not very probable, although the family were not altogether averse from this kind of canting or punning reference to their name. Collinson (iii. 341) gives the following inscription from a stone in Inglishcombe Church to one of the family, in after-years:

'This grave's a bed of roses; here doth ly
John Rosewell, gent, his wife, nine children, by.
Ætatis suæ 79. Ob^t 1no die Dec^r, Anno 1687.'

Burke, in his 'Armoury,' gives Rosewell ('Somerset, Wilts, and Devon,' *temp*. Conqueror): Pale gu. and ar. a lion rampant; and Rosewell, in his conveyance to Sir Henry Berkeley, seals with this seal.

'Book on the Axe,' says that this Sir Henry Rosewell was son of the Solicitor-General; but from a comparison of the dates it seems pretty clear that he was a grandson of the Solicitor-General, and son, rather than younger brother, of William Rosewell, the vendor of Yarlington, in 1592.

III.

YARLINGTON AND THE BERKELEYS,

From 1592 to the Death of Maurice Berkeley, Esq., January, 1673-74.

Sir Henry Berkeley, of Bruton, who purchased the Manor of Yarlington in February, 1592, was the son of Sir Maurice Berkeley, of Bruton, who was standard-bearer to Henry VIII., and a staunch adherent of his Vicar-General, the unscrupulous Cromwell, Henry's principal tool in the destruction of the monasteries; and Sir Maurice had been greatly enriched from these sources. The family was an offshoot of the great house of Berkeley, of Berkeley Castle, descended from a second son of Maurice, seventh Baron of Berkeley, *temp.* Edward II., whose eldest son, Thomas, eighth Baron, was owner of the castle at the time of the horrid death there of Edward II. Sir Maurice, of Bruton, had married, as his second wife, Elizabeth, daughter of Anthony Sandys, of Kent; and, by virtue of his will, she continued to reside at her husband's principal seat at Bruton; Sir Henry, the heir, meanwhile residing at Norwood Park, the lease of which Sir Maurice had obtained, after unavailing remonstrance, from the reluctant Abbot Whiting, the last and cruelly murdered Abbot of Glastonbury, by dint of sheer pressure, and certainly with Cromwell's sinister influence at his back. In Ellis's 'Letters' (vol. iii., 3rd series, p. 6, Lett. 258) there is an explanatory letter from the Abbot to Cromwell himself, in answer to his written desire, 'that I should indelayedly graunte unto your servaunte, Mr. Maurice Berkeley, under my Convente seal, the Maistershippe of the game, th' office of the Keper, and the herbage and pannage of my Parke of Northwode.' Perhaps Sir Henry had been a little nettled by this arrangement of his father's respecting Bruton; for by his own will, of date 30th May, 1600, he gives 'to his wife, Dame Margaret, for her jointure, the Manor-house of Bruton wherein he dwelt, *in as ample a manner* as his mother-in-law' (he means his step-mother) 'had the same, and his parsonages of Bruton, Bruham, Redlynch, Wick, Cole, Pitcombe, and Hatchpine,[1] and the tithes.'

'Item, I do give and bequeath to Harry Berkeley, my second son, all that my Manor of Yarlington, to him and his heirs for ever. Item, I do give to my son Harry all such household stuff as I shall have at my house at Yarlington at the time of my death.'

From this bequest it would appear that Sir Henry Berkeley, of Bruton, had occasionally used as a residence 'his house at Yarlington,' as well as his principal seat at Bruton; and, in fact, in a deed of conveyance of nine acres of land in Cary Moor, in 1601, he is described as Sir Henry Berkeley, of Yarlington, knight, and the land as 'lands which he had

---

[1] Hadspen, in Sir Henry Berkeley's will, is called 'Hatchpine,' in accordance with the barbarous pronunciation of the name which was universally prevalent in the neighbourhood up to within the last fifty years.

purchased, in 1582, of Robert Sedborough, of Gallington,[1] deceased.'

After the date of his will, viz., in 1601 (43 Elizabeth), by an indenture dated 27th August, and made between himself of the one part, and Henry Berkeley, gentleman, of the other part, Sir Henry covenants to stand seized of the Manor and advowson of Yarlington, and lands situate at Castle Cary, Bratton, Shepton Montague, and North Cadbury, ' all being lands known by the name of the Manor of Yarlington, and purchased by him of William Rosewell, esquire,' to the use of himself for life, remainder to his son Henry, in tail male, remainder to his heirs female in tail, remainder to Sir Henry's eldest son, Sir Maurice Berkeley, in tail male, with remainder to himself in fee. Power is reserved to Sir Henry to avoid this deed on payment of 5s. at the north porch of Bruton Church.

Sir Henry left at his decease three sons, viz.: Sir Maurice, his heir, Henry of Yarlington, and Edward.

To the last-named son, Edward, who became the ancestor of the Portmans, Sir Henry devised his estate of Pylle.

---

[1] By 'Gallington' in this deed is meant Galhampton. The place was very generally called 'Gallington,' in the corrupt pronunciation of the neighbourhood, in my youthful days. Galhampton is a very considerable hamlet comprised mainly in the parish of North Cadbury, but also, as to part, in the parish of Castle Cary. It abuts on the north-western boundary of Yarlington, and since the time of Sir Henry Berkeley has been much associated with that parish. It appears from Mr. Green's 'Somerset Charities' (Somerset Record Soc.), pp. 121, 304, that two acres of land lying in the fields of Galhampton within the parish of 'North Cadbury' were part of the possessions of Yarlington Church, rendering a 'rent of xvi^d.' for the use and maintenance of a light in the parish church 'there perpetually burning.' The expression, 'in the fields of Galhampton,' is not so vague or indefinite as at first sight appears. It applies to two large tracts of land in the hamlet of about forty acres, unenclosed until the beginning of this century, and known respectively as Galhampton Field, and North Field, being separated from each other by a road running through them east and west, leading from Yarlington to South Cary.

Collinson (vol. iii., p. 281) remarks of Maurice, the eldest son of Sir Henry Berkeley, and who was himself knighted in his father's lifetime, that 'by his wife Elizabeth, daughter of Sir John Killegrew, he had five sons, all knights.' Their names are given below.[1]

But we have now to confine ourselves to Henry Berkeley, Sir Henry's second son, who comes into possession of Yarlington at his father's decease, in 1602 or 1603. In a deed dated 6th August, 1603, he is described as Henry Berkeley, of Yarlington, esquire ; but at this time he was engaged in military service in Ireland — both he and his brother Maurice having attached themselves to the service of the Earl of Essex—and it is probable that he did not come into permanent residence at Yarlington until after his marriage, some years later.

However, in Michaelmas Term, 1606 (3 James I.), he suffered a recovery,[2] to Joseph Earth as demandant, of the Manor of Yarlington, and lands in Yarlington, Castle Cary, North Cadbury, Bratton, and Shepton Montague, and the advowson of Yarlington—with the object, of course, of barring the entail created by his father's deed of covenant of 1601.

---

[1] Sir Maurice Berkeley,=Elizabeth Killegrew. father of the five knights.

| Penelope Godolphin=Sir Charles. | Henry. | Maurice. | William, Admiral, killed at sea, 1666. | John, Lord Berkeley, of Stratton. |

[2] As the term 'recovery,' or 'common recovery,' will be of frequent recurrence, it may be as well to say here that it denotes the legal process—or solemnly constituted farce—by which the entail on an estate was *barred*, that is, enlarged into a fee simple, prior to 1834 ; when, by 3 and 4 Wm. IV., c. 74, 'simpler modes of assurance' were substituted for fines and recoveries.

Henry Berkeley married Elizabeth, one of the daughters of Sir Henry Neville, knight, and by an indenture dated 12th February, 1609 (being of the nature of a post-nuptial settlement), in which he is described as Henry Berkeley, of London, gentleman, of the one part, and Sir Wm. Killegrew, of Hanworth, county Middlesex, knight, and Henry Neville, esquire, son and heir-apparent of Sir Henry Neville, of Billingbere, in the county of Berks, of the other part, the said Henry Berkeley, in consideration of a competent jointure to be made unto Elizabeth Berkeley, now his wife, and for her increase of livelihood if she should happen to overlive the said Henry Berkeley, and *for the continuance of the lands and hereditaments in his name and blood* if he should die without issue of his body, thereby covenants with Killegrew and Neville, to stand seized of the Manor and advowson of Yarlington, to the use of himself and his wife Elizabeth, and the heirs of their bodies, with remainder to his younger brother Edward in tail, and with remainder to his eldest brother Sir Maurice in tail, with remainder to himself in fee.

Sir Henry Neville, of Billingbere, Berks, it may be said, was a brother of Edward, sixth Lord Abergavenny, and ancestor of the Lord Braybrookes. The Killegrews were already connected with the Berkeleys by the marriage of Elizabeth Killegrew with Henry Berkeley's eldest brother, Sir Maurice.

In connection with the desire, in the foregoing deed, expressed 'for the continuance of the lands in his name and blood,' it is interesting to note the avowal of a similar motive as influencing John, fifth Lord Berkeley of Stratton, and last male descendant of Sir Maurice, the elder brother of the covenantor in the above deed. Lord Berkeley, by his will in 1772, devised his valuable London property, consisting of Berkeley Square, Bruton Street, Stratton Street, etc., not to his nearest relatives on the female side, but to the very distantly related head of the Berkeleys, the Earl of Berkeley, of Berkeley Castle, in tail male, adding 'and all this I do, being the last male of my family, and desirous of nourishing the root from which it sprung, and wishing the stock may continue to flourish and put forth new branches as long as any form of civil government shall subsist in this country.' It is, however, to be noted, that although Lord Berkeley of Stratton, the testator, was 'the last male of his family,' as descended from Sir Maurice Berkeley, yet male descendants of Sir Maurice Berkeley's father, Sir Henry Berkeley of Bruton, were and are existing in the Portmans, as lineal male descendants of Edward Berkeley of Pylle, Sir Henry's third son. Possibly Lord Berkeley may have considered them as out of his purview, by reason of their having taken Portman as their surname, in lieu of Berkeley, or he may well have deemed that branch to be already so well 'nourished,' as to need no extraneous assistance whatever.

Soon after his post-nuptial settlement Henry Berkeley must have been knighted; for by a deed dated 30th May, 1612, the Rev. William Rosewell, of Yarlington, clerk, and Margaret his wife, convey to *Sir Henry Berkeley* of Yarlington, knight, and his heirs in fee simple, for £1,000, their interest in a messuage at Galhampton, *occupied by the said William Rosewell*, and their one-fourth share, or sixty-four acres, of Foxcombe Grounds, or the Manor of Foxcombe.

And from this time forward there is constant evidence of Sir Henry's living in the parish as a resident country gentleman, and perpetually busying himself in making additions to his property.

In 1613, in consideration of £90, Henry, Earl of Huntingdon, great grandson of Francis, Earl of Huntingdon, and Katharine Pole,[1] releases to Sir Henry Berkeley the annual rent-charge of £3 3s. 5½d., to which previous reference has been made (pp. 20, 25). In 1617 Sir Henry's eldest brother, Sir Maurice Berkeley of Bruton (father of the five knights) died, and Sir Henry then, by deed of 4th October, in the same year, purchases from his brother's widow, Dame Elizabeth Berkeley, Henry Bayntun, of Stavordale, gentleman, and Toby Pearce, of Bruton, gentleman, as executors of Sir Maurice, the residue of the renewable lease, for sixty years, of Smalldon Farm, consisting of 199 acres, which had been left to Sir Maurice by his father, Sir Henry of Bruton. The consideration for the purchase is £600. This property was afterwards the subject of considerable distraction to the Berkeley family.

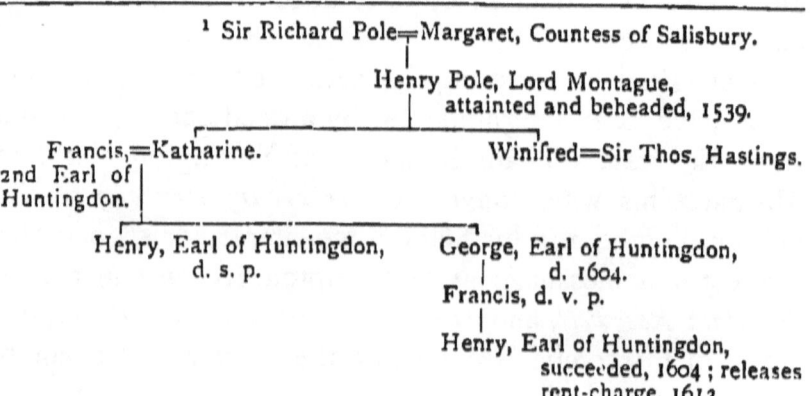

[1] Sir Richard Pole=Margaret, Countess of Salisbury.

In the same year, 1616-17, 9th February, but before the death of her eldest son Sir Maurice, the mother of the Berkeleys, 'Dame Margaret Berkeley, of Bruton, widdowe,' made her will; she, it will be remembered, was by her husband's will to enjoy the chief residence at Bruton, in as ample a manner as the stepmother had done. She leaves her eldest son, Sir Maurice, not only her household stuff at Bruton, but also such household stuff as remained at the lodge at Norwood Park (where Sir Maurice was living), 'praised at his father's death at £40, and now in Sir Maurice's possession.' She appoints as executors and residuary legatees her two sons, Sir Henry Berkeley, knight, and Edward Berkeley, esquire. Dame Margaret Berkeley, *née* Lygon, had married, as his second wife, Sir Thomas Russell of Strensham, whose widow she was when she married Sir Henry Berkeley; and she bequeaths 'to her son, Thomas Russell of Russhock, in the county of Wigorn, esquire,' one basin and ewer of silver, which was his father's, Sir Thomas Russell, deceased. She had a considerable dwelling-house, with a lodge, gardens, and orchards, at Wells, where she passed much of her time, and this property she directs to be sold to pay the very numerous and handsome legacies given by her will, many of them to residents at Wells. The will is attested by Henry Southworth,[1]

---

[1] Although the attesting witnesses of Dame Margaret Berkeley's will can have but very slight connection with the history of Yarlington, yet the names of two of them are of sufficient interest to the county of Somerset to justify a short reference to them. The third, William Cole, was her confidential servant, and a legatee under the will.

The Southworths were a family well settled in Wells. Thomas Southworth and Henry Southworth (the attesting witness) were two brothers residing there. Thomas Southworth was appointed Recorder of Wells, 1608-9, was M.P. for

Francis Cottington,[1] and William Cole. It is beautifully transcribed on three sheets of paper, and is endorsed in an easy running hand, with rather touching simplicity, 'My Mother's Will'—no doubt in the handwriting of Sir H. Berkeley, of Yarlington, one of the executors.

In 1629 a considerable prospective addition was made to

Wells in 1613 and again in 1619; he died in 1625. Henry Southworth was a great benefactor to the city of Wells. He was Lord of the Manor of Wyke Champflower, and rebuilt in a very handsome manner the chapel of ease there, abutting on the manor-house. He had two daughters co-heiresses: Jane, who married William Bull, of Shapwick, by which marriage the Manor of Wyke passed by descent to Mr. H. Bull-Strangways, who some twenty-five or thirty years ago sold it to the principal tenant, Mr. Mullins; Margaret, the other daughter, married Dr. Arthur Ducke, a very celebrated civilian of his day, who was Chancellor of the Diocese of Bath and Wells, and also of London, and M.P. for Minehead in 1640. Henry Southworth died the same year as his brother, the Recorder, and was buried at Wyke in May, 1625.

[1] Francis Cottington can be none other than Sir Francis Cottington, afterwards (in 1631) Lord Cottington of Hanworth, who fills so large a space in Clarendon's History, and who (*temp.* Commonwealth) went with Hyde from the Hague to Spain on an embassy from Charles II., Cottington then being seventy-five years old. Laud, Stafford, and Cottington had been the three principal and most intimate advisers of Charles I.; and it is said that the term 'Cabinet Ministers' was first applied to these three Ministers, on account of their joint and close influence with the Sovereign. The Cottingtons had been for many generations settled at Godminster, in the parishes of Pitcombe and Bruton. Clarendon says of Lord Cottington: 'He was born a gentleman both by father and mother; his father having a pretty entire estate near Bruton, in Somersetshire, worth about £200 a year, which had descended from father to son for many hundred years, and is still in possession of his elder brother's children, the family having been always Roman Catholic. His mother was a Stafford, nearly allied to Sir E. Stafford, Vice-Chamberlain to Queen Elizabeth, by whom this gentleman had been brought up.' According to another account (Lodge's 'Illustrious Personages'), his mother was Jane Byfleet, the daughter of a country gentleman of that name living in the neighbouring parish of Bratton Seymour. 'Utram harum mavis, accipe.' Many of the Cottingtons were buried in Pitcombe Church. Lord Cottington himself died at Valladolid, in 1652, having obtained permission from Charles to remain in Spain, where he had spent many years of his early life in connection with various embassies. At Valladolid he declared himself a Roman Catholic, and his epitaph in the Jesuits' Church there concluded with an expression of his will that 'his body be deposited in this temple till such time as God restored to his Church the kingdom of England.' 'In May, 1678' (says Kennet), 'his bones were brought over to England upon a prospect of popery coming in about that time.'

Sir Henry Berkeley's estate, by a conveyance from Roger Earth, of Dinton, in Wilts, of the capital mansion of Brooks Court and estate, in Ilchester (let shortly afterwards to a Mr. Giles Raymond for £120 per year) to Henry Bayntun, of Roundhill, gentleman, and another, in trust for the use of the settlor, Roger Earth, for life ; then for Joseph Earth, the son of the Rev. Wm. Earth, of Mildenhall, Wilts, clerk, deceased, for life ; remainder to Sir Henry Berkeley, in fee, with a proviso that, if Joseph should impeach Roger Earth's will, the trustees should stand possessed of the property to the use of his executor. And by his will, dated 21st January, 1630-31, and proved in the Prerogative Court, 16th May, 1634, Roger Earth made 'his beloved friend, Sir Henry Berkeley, his executor and residuary legatee.' And on the 19th May, 1634, Joseph Earth, described as of Ramsbury, Wilts, and Sir Henry Berkeley, gave bonds to each other to abide by the award of William, Earl of Hertford. This William, Earl of Hertford, was great-grandson of the Protector Somerset, and he was restored to the title of Duke of Somerset in 1660.

The family of the Earths, so far as I have been able to unearth them, consisted at this time of three brothers, viz. :

Joseph Earth,	Roger Earth,	The Rev. William Earth,
of High Holborn,	of Dinton,	of Mildenhall, clerk,
d. 1609.	d. 1634.	d. before 1629.
		Joseph Earth,
		of Ramsbury, gent.

Burke, in his 'Armoury,' gives 'Earth (Dinton, co. Wilts), argent three stags' heads, couped sa., attired or.'

Brooks Court, or Place, was the cradle of the family of Brook, Lord Cobham, from *temp.* Henry III., as given in

Collinson (vol. iii., p. 302), who adds that it was inhabited by Wm. Brook, Lord Cobham, Ambassador to France (1 Elizabeth); and that his son Henry, Lord Cobham, succeeding him (39 Elizabeth), was attainted and his estates forfeited to James I., for being concerned with Sir Walter Raleigh and Lord Grey of Wilton, in the alleged conspiracy against the King for the purpose of setting the Lady Arabella Stuart on the throne, and that he died, in 1619, in great poverty.[1]

After the attainder of Henry, Lord Cobham, Joseph Earth, of High Holborn, became possessed of Brooks Court, whether by direct purchase, or whether in consideration of moneys advanced or services rendered to James I., does not appear. Joseph Earth has already (p. 31) been mentioned as demandant to Henry Berkeley's recovery of 1606, and probably he was an attorney; all that does appear is, that by his will, dated 17th February, 1609, and proved in the Prerogative Court, 9th September, 1609, this Joseph Earth, of High Holborn, devised Brooks Court, in Somerset, to his brother Roger in fee. Joseph Earth the younger was probably of weak intellect, and Sir Henry Berkeley was to look after him; there was no provision for any eventual marriage. In 1636 Sir Henry Berkeley leases portions of Brooks Court estate, and thenceforth deals with it as his own property.

---

[1] This mysterious plot in 1603 has never been elucidated. Two Roman Catholic priests were executed, as was George Brook, brother of Lord Cobham. Lord Cobham himself was attainted, and all his estates forfeited. Raleigh, the most accomplished man of his age, was kept in confinement for thirteen years. Sir Edward Coke, afterwards a flaming patriot and Liberal, conducted the case for the Crown against Raleigh, and with even more than his usual virulence denounced him as 'a traitor,' 'a monster,' 'a viper,' 'a spider of hell.' It was with reference to Raleigh's long imprisonment that Prince Henry remarked, 'Sure, no king but my father would keep such a bird in a cage.'

PEDIGREE OF BERKELEY, OF BRUTON AND YARLINGTON.

```
CATHERINE, ═(1) Sir Maurice ═(2) Elizabeth,
daughter of Wm. Blount,        daughter of Antony Sandys,
Lord Mountjoy.                 of Kent.
           │
           SIR HENRY BERKELEY, ┬ Margaret (née) Lygon,
           of Bruton (purchased Yar-    widow as his second wife of Sir Thomas
           lington, 1592; will dated    Russell, of Strensham.
           30th May, 1600).
           │
   ┌───────┴──────────────────────────────┐
Sir Maurice Berkeley, ┬ Elizabeth Killigrew.   SIR HENRY BERKELEY ┬ Elizabeth Neville,   Edward Berkeley,
of Bruton, five sons                           of Yarlington, m. 1608-9;   d. 1656-57.    of Pylle, ances-
all knights.                                   will dated, 1663; d. 1667.                 tor of the Port-
   │                                              │                                        mans.
Penelope Godolphin ═ Sir Charles. Henry. Maurice. William. John,
   │                                              Admiral,  Baron
   │                                              killed at  Berkeley,
   │                                              sea,1666.  of Strat-
   │                                                         ton.
   │                                              │
   │                             ┌────────────────┴──────────┐
   │                         DOROTHY ═ Sir Francis Godolphin,   Frances ┬ Peter Roynon,
   │                                   m. cir. 1631.                       m. 1655.
   │                                                                    │
MAURICE,  JAEL,  Margaret,                                              ┌────┴────────┐
of Yarlington,  d. 1705.  d. 1659.                                    Peter,        HARRY ROYNON,
d. 1673.                                                              ob. infans.    b. 1658.
   │
SIR WILLIAM GODOLPHIN,  Sidney, Lord Godolphin.   Henry Godolphin, D.D.,
created a Baronet, 1661; died                     Provost of Eton.
17th August, 1710.
```

Although we are now reaching the period of the Great Rebellion, in which many of his nephews, sons of his deceased brother Sir Maurice, took such a strenuous and decided part on behalf of the Crown, yet Sir Henry himself, whether by reason of advancing years or from natural disinclination, appears to have kept himself entirely aloof, and altogether free from any engagements in connection with either side.

In 1648 he grants a lease of the tolls of Yarlington Fair[1] for fifty shillings, payable 16th August, ten days in advance. At this period the family of this prosperous knight consisted of one son, Maurice, and four daughters, Jael, Dorothy, Margaret, and Frances. His second daughter, Dorothy,[2] was married to Sir Francis Godolphin, with which family the Berkeleys were already connected through the Killegrews, and also by the marriage of Sir Charles Berkeley, Sir Maurice's eldest son and Sir Henry's eldest nephew, with Penelope Godolphin, sister of Sir Francis.

In 1665 a marriage is arranged between Frances Berkeley and Peter Roynon, Esq., and Sir Henry agrees to advance a sum of £1,200. The Roynons, or Ronyons,

---

[1] This fair, held on 26th August, was, during a lengthened period, largely attended, and of constantly increasing importance, until, in quite recent times, it became altogether superseded by the modern and more rational system of market-day auctions, and of periodical repository sales of live stock, held for the convenience of purchasers, at the principal railway centres. Falling at a season when the weather is usually more settled for fair than at any other time of the year, it formed an epoch in the local calendar, giving rise to a proverbial saying known to all the country-side: 'The first rain after Yarlington Fair brings winter.'

[2] Bishop Wilberforce, in his second and fifth tables of pedigrees attached to 'Evelyn's Life of Mrs. Godolphin,' published in 1847, gives Dorothy Berkeley as the daughter of Sir *Charles* Berkeley of Yarlington; and it was with a view to correct this error that I was first led at that time to examine the old Yarlington documents in my father's possession.

were a good Somersetshire family, originally of Shepton Mallet and West Harptree. The Smalldon renewable leases for sixty years, now possessed by Sir Henry Berkeley, had been, just 150 years before (viz., in 1505), originally granted by Adrian, Bishop of Bath and Wells, subject to a rent of £9, to Richard Ronyon, of Shepton Mallet, who by his will bequeathed the same to the church of Shepton Mallet, to the intent that the churchwardens might pray for the souls of the said Richard, and Agnes his wife, and all faithful defunct. The churchwardens had entered on the land as wardens and trustees of Ronyon's Charity, and sold the leases in 1535 to Chief Justice Fitz-James, of Redlynch, and Elizabeth his wife, subject to the payment of the rent of £9 to the Bishop, and of £6 6s. 8d. to the Chantry Wardens of Shepton Mallet for the sustenance of the chapel. Smalldon itself, or Smalldown, as it is now called, is a farm of 200 acres, on very high ground to the north of Evercreech, to which parish it belongs. Well, the marriage of Miss Frances Berkeley with Peter Roynon, Esq., duly took place, and on 2nd December, 1656, a little Peter Roynon was baptized in Yarlington Church, to be followed in due time by another boy, Harry.

But now deaths are beginning to occur. Dame Elizabeth Berkeley is buried at Yarlington, 4th January, 1656-57, just one month after the birth of her grandson, Peter Roynon; and two years after, in 1659, Margaret, the third daughter (named, of course, after her grandmother, Dame Margaret of Bruton), is also buried there. His youngest daughter, Frances Roynon, then dies in Sir Henry Berkeley's lifetime. And at last, on 31st August, 1667, the parish register records the death and burial of Sir Henry himself, having 'overlived' his wife, Dame Elizabeth, more than ten years. He must himself, at his death, have been very close upon ninety years of age. He had made his will in 1663. In this will, so far as his lands are concerned, he says :

> 'I give to my son, Maurice Berkeley, all my lands, goods, and whatsoever is mine unbequeathed. But my will is, that if my son shall, by God's good pleasure, departe this life without lawful issue, that then my daughter Jael shall have my estate at Ivelchester; my daughter Dorothy and her heirs by Sir Francis Godolphin my estate at Yarlington, Galhampton, and Foxcombe; my daughter Frances my estate at Babcary, Smalldown, and Bratton Lines.'

By Sir Henry's death the family residing at Yarlington are now reduced to his son, Maurice, and his eldest daughter, Jael, or Madam Jael Berkeley, as she is afterwards generally designated; and as Sir Henry's post-nuptial settlement was made in February, 1609-10, it is reasonable to suppose that she was now nearing sixty years of age.

As no executor was named in Sir Henry's will, administration with the will annexed was granted to his son Maurice by the Prerogative Court, on the 7th of September, 1667—in fact, just seven days after his father's funeral. Now, of this son, Maurice, we have absolutely no information whatever as to what he was doing in his father's lifetime. His cousins, Sir Charles and Sir John, sons of his uncle Sir Maurice, had been deeply engaged for the royal cause; but of this particular Maurice Berkeley nothing whatever is known to the writer.

As we have seen, he loses no time in taking out administration to his father, and he immediately sets to work at letting out his lands for high premiums, instead of at a yearly rack-rent. In November, 1667, the year of his father's death, he grants a lease of Foxcombe to one John Lewis for a fine of £700; in the following year he leases another part of Foxcombe for a fine of £50. In 1670 he renews, for a fine of £60, a lease to John Clothier of 34½ acres, part of Foxcombe, originally leased to him by Sir Henry Berkeley in 1651. In 1671 he leases 18 acres of Foxcombe, for a fine of £110 and a rent of 16s., to John Robbins, *alias* Syms. He had also mortgaged the Ilchester property (Brooks Court) to a Mr. Mildmay for £500, and on 2nd January, 1673-74, he dies intestate, and is buried at Yarlington on 8th January.

It is evident that Maurice's reign of six years, if short, had been disastrous. It looks very much as if he were merely a thriftless loon engaged in raising money to pay obligations he had incurred in his father's lifetime. Sir Henry had left by his will a sum of £2,000 to his daughter Jael as her fortune; £1,050, part of this sum, consisted of certain specified mortgages and securities which Sir Henry held, and the remaining £950 was charged on the Galhampton and Foxcombe estates, which he devised to his son Maurice. Of this £950, it appears that Maurice had paid off £150, leaving at his death the remaining £800, secured by his bond to Jael. There does not seem to have been any other charge left by Sir Henry's will, and the condition in which Maurice's affairs were found to be at his death seems only to be accounted for by his own improvidence.

There are only two facts which occur to the writer as worthy of notice with regard to him. First, that at his decease his principal available assets (as we shall presently see) consisted of farming stock, sheep, and oxen; from whence the inference may be drawn that upon succeeding to the estate he had engaged pretty largely in those agricultural pursuits in which country gentlemen are often tempted to embark with more or less—and generally less than more —success; and, secondly, it is observable that the field in which his operations for raising money were carried on seems to have been limited to the various outlying properties which had come to him from his father; there being no evidence that he had in any way encumbered his Manor of Yarlington.

However, the male line of the Berkeleys of Yarlington is now extinct, and henceforth Madam Jael Berkeley alone represents the family at Yarlington—a woman of superlative strength of will, of extraordinary energy, and of the most indomitable resolution.

IV.

MADAM JAEL BERKELEY,

(HER TRIALS AND TRIUMPHS):

THE ROYNONS AND GODOLPHINS, FROM 1673 TO 1712.

MR. WALTER SHANDY, as we know, in the early part of last century, propounded the philosophical theory, 'that a great deal more depended upon names than what superficial minds were capable of conceiving.' It was Mr. Shandy's declared opinion 'that there was a strange kind of magic bias which what he called good or bad names irresistibly impressed upon our character and conduct.' Now, it is tolerably certain that, if Mr. Shandy could have been aware of the circumstances and the conduct of Jael Berkeley, he would at once have claimed her as an apt illustration of his philosophical theory. Without going into the question of the goodness or badness of the name, it is undoubtedly a peculiar name; and the Shandean theory would have unquestionably broken down if a lady of the name of Jael had been other than a person of considerable determination and decision of character—one who, having a doubtful and difficult task before her, would address herself to the despatch of business without flinching, and who would knock the nail on the head in a thorough and workmanlike manner. And so it was with Jael[1] Berkeley.

In the first place, as a security for her claim of £800 in her late brother's hands, she obtains administration from the Prerogative Court on 23rd of February, the month following her brother's death; and Sir Henry Berkeley's will is at once submitted to the celebrated Serjeant Maynard for his opinion 'as to the estates taken by the three sisters, now that their brother Maurice has died without issue.' Serjeant Maynard is well known as the great legal authority at the time of the Revolution, some fifteen years after this. Jointly with Somers, he took a prominent part in the convention which had to settle the terms on which William should take on the regal government. He was then ninety years old, and on being introduced to the Prince, William addressed him, 'Well, Mr. Serjeant, you must have survived all the lawyers of your time.'

'Yes, your Highness,' said Maynard; 'and if you had not been pleased to come to our aid, I believe I should soon have survived all the laws as well.'

Serjeant Maynard, whose autograph opinion with the 'case' is now before me, says 'Jael takes Ilchester in fee, Frances Smalldon in fee, and Dorothy an estate tail in Yarlington.' But the 'case' submitted to Serjeant Maynard omitted the important fact that Frances Roynon had died in her father's lifetime.

Meanwhile sore troubles are crowding round Madam Jael. Maurice's creditors were clamorous on every side, and even before taking out administration to his effects she had sold

---

[1] The name is spelt indifferently Jael and Jaell.

'many sheep and oxen of Maurice's to the value of £120,' to appease the more pressing of them ; and in order to stay an action against herself, had paid a debt of his of £83. Her sister Dorothy, and her husband, Sir Francis Godolphin, are now both dead, and Sir William Godolphin, as their eldest son and heir, proceeded to file a bill—no doubt a friendly bill—in Chancery against Jael Berkeley, his aunt, and against young Peter Roynon (now eighteen), the infant son of Frances Berkeley and Peter Roynon, to establish their respective rights under Sir Henry Berkeley's will ; while Peter Roynon, the father, on his part, in right of his eldest son, had already entered bodily ' on the ground called Smalldon,' and had cut a turf there, and had forbidden the tenant to pay any rent to Jael as the administratrix of her brother Maurice—Smalldon, as we have seen, being a leasehold, or chattel real.

But now comes a really extraordinary incident.

Sir William Godolphin, as has been said, had instituted a family suit in Chancery to give effect to Sir Henry Berkeley's will, to which Jael and the Roynons put in separate answers, when the Roynons discover, for the first time, the post-nuptial settlement of 1609, sixty-five years old (of which previous mention has been hereinbefore frequently made), by which Sir Henry Berkeley had made a settlement of Yarlington on his heirs in tail general. Consequently the devise in his will of Yarlington, to Dorothy, was of none effect; and, *under the will*, Sir William Godolphin only becomes entitled in tail to the lands at Galhampton and Foxcombe, acquired by Sir Henry after the settlement of 1609. He therefore ceases to go on with the suit, and Jael, in perplexity, submits a fresh case to Mr. William Jones (afterwards Sir William Jones, and Attorney-General to Charles II.), a lawyer of great eminence, as to her interests generally, 'now this last entayled deed hath appeared, for it hath been lately found.' The deed had been in the custody of the Nevilles, Dame Elizabeth Berkeley's brothers; and she herself having been now long dead, it had been entirely lost sight of by Sir Henry Berkeley, or regarded by him as a nullity. Indeed, so completely had the deed been ignored by both Sir Henry and his wife, that so long back as 1633 they had taken quite unnecessary steps to repeat what that settlement had already effected; for by a deed of 1st July, in that year, between Sir Henry and Dame Elizabeth of the one part, and Edward Biss, of Spargrove, esquire, Henry Bayntun, of Roundhill, esquire, and John Lovell, of Shepton Montague, gentleman, of the other part, the Berkeleys demise Yarlington for ninety-nine years to the three others as trustees, with intent to levy a fine, and, subject thereto, to the use of Sir Henry for life, remainder to Dame Elizabeth for life, remainder to the right heirs of Sir Henry Berkeley. And in Trinity Term of the same year a fine is levied accordingly; the object being simply to make that very provision for Dame Elizabeth, 'if she should happen to overlive her husband,' which had already been secured to her by the post-nuptial indenture of 1609. And independently of this action on their part, it is certainly matter for comment, if the genuineness of this deed had been in question, first, that Henry Berkeley's wife was not a party to it; and, secondly, that Henry Berkeley himself, who, if not at the time resident at Yarlington, had nevertheless for several years been recognised, in all deeds and documents, as 'Henry Berkeley, of Yarlington, esquire,' should have received so vague and indefinite a description therein as 'Henry Berkeley, of London, gentleman.'

However, Mr. Robert Neville now produces a deed which he declares to be a true 'copy of the original, then remaining in his possession. This identical attested copy, examined with the original 8th June, 1674, is now lying before me, as no doubt, 215 years ago, it was laid before Sir William Jones, to accompany the 'case.' Sir William Jones, it may be observed, was a Somersetshire man, a son of Richard Jones, of Stowey and Chew Magna, and a neighbour of the Roynons of West Harptree. The original 'case' and 'opinion,' dated 7th November, 1674, with thirteen questions affecting Jael's duties and interests in this state of affairs, with Jones's answers to each question, is in my possession, and is a most exhaustive document. One of the questions relates to a very old matter—the effect of the common recovery, suffered by Sir Henry, in 1606, to Joseph Earth—and the point was whether he had effectually cut off the entail, created by Sir Henry the father under the deed of covenant of 1601: 'there being no Deed to be found to lead to the uses of the said Recovery, nor any Deed or Fine to make a Tenant to the Præcipe'? And Jones answers: 'I think the intayle was well cut off, for though there was no Deed to lead to the uses, the law implies a use to Sir Henry and his heirs, and you needed not deed or fine to make a tenant to the præcipe, if the præcipe were brought against Henry, who was tenant in tail in possession.'

On the general question as to Yarlington, Jones is of opinion that 'Yarlington being entayled' (*i.e.*, by the deed of 1609) 'doth descend to the heirs of the body of Henry and Elizabeth Berkeley, so that Jael and the two sons of her two deceased sisters have equal right to the Manor, as coparceners in tail.'

Sir William Godolphin, therefore, only gets, under Sir Henry's will, the lands at Galhampton and Foxcombe, and Jael, as the person chiefly benefited by the will, is recommended to prove it by examination of witnesses in Chancery.

Another question was, 'As to the land at Ivelchester' (Brooks Court), 'which was given to Jael by her father, by his last will, which it appears was mortgaged by her brother to a Mr. Mildmay, for £500. Mr. Mildmay hath not entered upon the land, but hath forbidden the tenant to pay the Rent to Jael.' What course shall a distracted Jael take in this case for the recovery of the rent? Answer: 'If the father gave the land' (to Jael), 'the Mortgage will be void. But the Mortgagee may have remedy on his bond or covenant, if there be assetts.'

Another subject which was a cause of uneasiness to Jael, was in reference to her own position as regarded Maurice's debts. She had not only taken out administration with a view to obtain priority for her own debt of £800, secured by Maurice's bond, but even before administration had dealt with the intestate's goods, selling (as we have seen) many of his sheep and oxen, to satisfy his more clamorous creditors, thereby constituting herself what is called in law 'executrix of her own wrong.' And a question in the case was, whether this would make her liable beyond the goods of Maurice which came into her hands and were fully accounted for.

To which Jones makes answer: 'She will be no further liable than the goods she took into her hands will amount to. Therefore if she have paid to the value of the goods, there is no question but she is safe.' But as to the securing priority for her own debt, Jones sees that here 'a difficulty will arise.' 'When she did, before administration taken, administer as executrix of her own wrong, and did after take out administration, yet she may be sued still, as executrix of her own wrong, and then she cannot retayne for her own debt.'[1]

But now comes the crucial point as to Smalldon. 'Smalldon is a chattel lease, and was given by Sir Henry Berkeley, in his will, to his daughter Frances, she dying before the will took effect. *Quære*, whether shall this go to the payment of the debts of the said Maurice, or to the administrator of Frances?'

'It cannot go to Frances, but will go to Maurice' (that is, it had lapsed), 'to whom the residue of the estate of Sir Henry was devised, and so will be assetts as to Maurice's debts.'

Again: 'Whether the heirs of Frances, she dying before the will took effect, have right to any more than the third part of the land which was given to Frances by the will of

---

[1] 'For otherwise the creditors of the deceased would be running a race to take possession of his goods, without taking administration to him.'—Coulter's Case—Williams Executors, vol. i., 198, 3rd edition.

Sir H. Berkeley, her father, viz., at Babcary and Bratton Lines?'

Answer: 'The devise to Frances being void, the lands intended to be devised do descend, and her issue have but a third part by descent, there being three sisters.

'(Signed)   W. JONES, 7th Nov., /74.'

Here, then, is a triumphant result for Madam Jael. With the exception of Galhampton and Foxcombe, which go to her nephew Sir William Godolphin, she alone of the three sisters takes any benefit under the will. Yarlington, which was devised to the Godolphins, being governed by the entail general of the post-nuptial settlement, passes to the three sisters or their heirs in tail; viz., one-third to Jael, one-third to Sir William Godolphin, and one-third to young Peter Roynon, which last third, however, passes on to Harry Roynon on the death, under age, of his elder brother Peter. Jael takes the estate at Ilchester (Brooks Court) under the devise. Babcary (an estate of sixty-six acres, bought by Sir H. Berkeley of Francis Petre, esq.) and Bratton, having been devised to Frances, have lapsed, and this portion of the property passes to the three sisters or their heirs, as coparceners in fee, as the heirs of their brother Maurice; while Smalldon, in which the too impetuous Mr. Roynon had cut a premature turf in right of the devise to his wife, being a chattel lease, vests wholly in Jael, as administratrix of her brother Maurice, and as assets in her hand for the payment of his numberless debts.

The parties now, therefore, settle down to their respective rights. In less than six months after the 'case' and 'opinion,' Jael, 'as administratrix of her brother Maurice,' by indenture dated 14th April, 1675, assigns for £300 the Smalldon estate to the Rev. Joseph Barker, of Sherborne. Sir Henry Berkeley had renewed the lease, in the form of a lease for ninety-nine years, determinable on three lives, and it was now determinable on Jael's life, as the last of the three sisters, his daughters, whom Sir Henry had named as the lives in taking out his renewal. Moreover, Jael, as the eldest of the coparceners, having claim to the first presentation to the living, enters into a contemporaneous arrangement, that one of the Rev. Joseph's sons by Katherine, his then wife, shall be admitted to the Rectory at the first vacancy at her disposal; and on 12th June a bond passes between herself and Barker, in a sum of £500, for the more effectually emphasising this stipulation.

I am afraid that our modern Church reformers, who seem desirous that all presentations should be at the absolute disposal of the Bishop, or, still worse, of some Diocesan Board of Presentations, if not of our all-sufficient County Councils, will turn up the whites of their eyes at this transaction. Possibly Madam Jael Berkeley took a simple matter-of-fact view of the whole arrangement, under the impression that if she could do a good turn as well to herself as to Barker (and Katherine Barker, from the special introduction of her name, was probably also some female friend), no great harm would be done by killing two birds, as it were, with one stone; having regard also to the fact that whoever was nominated must be, after all, a fully qualified person in holy orders, and duly accepted by the Bishop, before admission to the preferment. But it is also extremely probable that, like her Kenite namesake, our Jael, having an object of paramount importance in view—that of getting free from her brother Maurice's entanglements—was not over-squeamish as to the means of attaining her end. The outlook for the Rev. Joseph Barker's son was certainly speculative rather than cheerful, as Jael herself was getting into years, and her brother Maurice had so lately as the September of the previous year presented one John Randall, A.B., to the living. Barker himself died about two years after this, and the Rev. John Randall having also happened to die in 1679, Joseph Barker, the son, is duly instituted to the Rectory on the 2nd of August in that year, 'by Katherine Barker, by reason of Jael Berkeley, as daughter of Sir Henry Berkeley, having granted the advowson to the said Katherine's husband, Joseph Barker.'[1] Joseph Barker, the son, held the living for forty-four years, until his death in 1723, and, it may be hoped, without offence or any injury to his usefulness as a parish priest, by reason of the conditions affecting his presentation.

But the year before his appointment to Yarlington, viz., by deed of 30th May, 1678, Jael was enabled, by repayment of the sum of £300, to obtain from Katherine Barker, as 'widow and administratrix of Joseph Barker, late of Sherborne, deceased,' the reassignment to herself of the Smalldon estate. Thus we see that, in the space of four years from her brother Maurice's death, Jael had emerged from all her difficulties, and had cleared off her brother's debts; and we may have good hope that the too-

---

[1] Mr. Weaver's 'Somerset Incumbents,' p. 226: Yarlington.

confiding Mr. Mildmay recovered his doubtfully-secured loan of £500, with all lawful interest.

Madam Jael has now no occasion to betake herself to Brooks Court, which her father had left her for a residence; she remains at the old Manor-house as the representative of the Berkeleys, and was buried at Yarlington in extreme old age, 26th September, 1705, being duly entered in the parish register as 'Madam Jael Berkeley.' Her father, as we have seen, must have been pretty well on ninety at his death, and Jael herself must have had quite as long a life, and the whole of it passed in the parish of Yarlington.[1]

It has been mentioned that Harry Roynon, described as of Lincoln's Inn, had succeeded his brother Peter in the right to the third share of Yarlington. But Jael had very little to do with the Roynons; she ever resented that cutting of the turf on Smalldon Hill by Peter, the father.

There are many transactions between her and Sir William Godolphin, all tending to secure to him Jael's share and interest in Yarlington and her estate of Brooks Court, to the exclusion of the Roynons. Thus, by indenture, dated

---

[1] The old monument of stone, with the Berkeley arms, on the south side of the chancel, whose record had become illegible even when Collinson wrote, had probably been erected by Jael Berkeley and Sir William Godolphin to the memory of Sir Henry Berkeley and Dame Elizabeth his wife, both buried at Yarlington; while the canopy, which in 1822, on the rebuilding of the chancel by the then Rector, Canon Frankland, had been absurdly placed over the chancel door, was at my suggestion restored as a sort of cenotaph to the chancel in the renovation of 1878, although now on the north side. The stone in the chancel floor, noticed both by Collinson and Phelps, as inscribed to the memory of the Rev. Richard Gapper, A.B., 'a worthy parish priest and sincere honest man,' has been (I say it with grief and shame) transferred to outside the church porch, where it is fast becoming obliterated by the effects of the weather and the feet of the church-goers, so slight—or so slighted—appear to have been the precautions taken in the faculties issued by my immediate predecessors in the Chancellorship of the Diocese!

15th January, 1679, between Jael Berkeley of the first part, Sir William Godolphin, baronet, of the second part, and Charles Godolphin, esquire, of the third part, Jael Berkeley, for the love and affection which she did bear unto the said William Godolphin her nephew, did convey all her lands in Galhampton and Foxcombe, and her third part of the Manor of Yarlington, to Charles Godolphin and his heirs, to the use of Jael Berkeley for life, with remainder to the use of Sir William Godolphin, his heirs and assigns.

This was followed by an agreement, dated 1st October, 1693, between her and Sir William Godolphin, by which it was arranged that he should grant her an annuity of £300 a year for life, and should receive from her a conveyance in fee of Brooks Court, or Place, of Galhampton, Foxcombe, and of her one-third of Yarlington, and her interest in the lease of Smalldon, which now remained on her life alone, but with power to her to inhabit two-thirds of Yarlington House, and to cut necessary fuel, which agreement was during the same month carried out by various deeds.

And in 1696 a lease was granted for three years by Sir William Godolphin and Harry Roynon of Yarlington Farm, *except* the mansion-house, fish-ponds and gardens, for £170 a year, the rents received being £113 6s. 8d. to Godolphin, and £56 13s. 4d. to Roynon.

The Roynons, as has been said, were a well-established family in the county, and at this time were connected by marriage with the Spekes of Jordans, as well as with the Berkeleys. Peter Roynon himself seems to have been an efficient county magistrate, and in 1685, after the battle of Sedgmoor—'there being many poor prisoners taken in or

for the late rebellion in the West, and committed to custody
in the cloisters of the cathedral church, and in the parish
church of St. Cuthbert in Wells, and also in several other
places there'—he was named on a committee, or com-
mission, with three other persons, the Right Hon. Francis
Poulett, Edward Berkeley, Esq., and John Bailey, Doctor
of Laws, ' four of his Majesty's justices of the peace of the
said county ' (of Somerset), to investigate the charges for the
maintenance of these prisoners, and to rectify and adjust
the several accounts of such charges, ' and the true state of
the same accounts, when so rectified and adjusted, humbly
to certify the same unto his Majesty, under their or any
two or more of their hands, in writing.'[1] But young Harry
Roynon, the son, Jael Berkeley's nephew, was evidently no
credit to the family. Coming of age and into his share of
the property in 1679, he suffers, in Hilary Term, 1685, a
common recovery to John Davis,[2] of Wells, gentleman, of
his ' one-third share of the Manor and advowson of Yarlington,' the uses of which recovery he declares, by an
indenture of the 18th July following, between himself,
described as Harry Roynon, esquire, of Lincoln's Inn, and
George Dodington, esquire, of Wells, to be to himself in fee.
Immediately after this he commences a series of assign-
ments by way of mortgage of his share. During the next
five years there are eleven such deeds for various sums

---

[1] Serel's ' Church of St. Cuthbert in Wells,' p. 32.
[2] This John Davis, a solicitor, of Wells, married Margaret, a daughter of
Christopher Dodington, Recorder of Wells, a member of which family is the
George Dodington, of Wells, esquire, party to the deed declaring the uses of the
recovery. John Davis was four times Mayor of Wells, in 1672, 1679, 1689 and
1690. He was father of Peter Davis, Esq., barrister, Recorder of Wells (1705),
and a Bencher of Lincoln's Inn.

thus borrowed by him from various persons, and at length, in 1701, Sir William Godolphin pays off the encumbrances by buying up the share for £1,815. And Jael Berkeley is not only relieved from all anxiety as to her uninterrupted enjoyment of Roynon's one-third share of the Manor-house, but has the inexpressible satisfaction of living long enough to see her father's Manor of Yarlington and his other property, all of which had been the subject of so much dissension and of such conflicting interests, preserved from threatened dissipation, and altogether consolidated, and in the good keeping of a worthy owner. And in this rather ignominious manner Harry Roynon quits the scene, so far as Yarlington is concerned; to reappear, however, in shadowy and spectral guise after an interval of some 120 or 130 years, when (about 1827) a certain Peter Roynon Lewis, a gentleman employed as a clerk in some Government office in town (Excise or Audit, I rather think), came down from London to call upon my father, with the object of obtaining from him, as a Governor of Christ's Hospital, a promise for a nomination for a son, on the strength of his claim as a lineal descendant and legal representative of Harry Roynon, formerly of Yarlington!

As regards Sir William Godolphin, who lived and died a bachelor at his seat in Cornwall, I would record one small matter. It has been mentioned that Maurice Berkeley, in 1670, for a fine of £60, renewed to one John Clothier, of Woolston, a lease of thirty-four and a half acres, part of Foxcombe, which had originally been granted to the same John Clothier, in 1651, by Sir Henry Berkeley; and it is pleasant, and speaks well for all parties, to be able to add that on 1st August, 1686, Sir William Godolphin renews this lease to *William* Clothier, ' in consideration of his good service to Maurice Berkeley, esquire, uncle of Sir William Godolphin.' What those services were, who can say? Whether he had served under Maurice in the wars, or had done him a good turn at a pinch in his money difficulties, is nowhere recorded.

Sir William Godolphin's next brother, Sidney Godolphin, the second son of Dorothy Berkeley and Sir Francis Godolphin, was the well-known courtier, of whom Charles II. remarked, in his witty phrase, ' that he was never in the way, and never out of the way.' After filling the highest offices of State, he had been made a peer with the title of Baron Godolphin, and was created Earl of Godolphin in 1706. He died in 1712, leaving a son, Francis, second Earl of Godolphin, who had succeeded to the Manor and estate two years before, under the will of his uncle, Sir William Godolphin.

There is little more of personal interest in connection with the devolution of the Manor. It was originally, as we have seen, the appanage of a very great family, the Barons of Montacute, then of the Nevilles, the Plantagenets, and the Parrs; and it now once more passes into high ducal families; Francis, second Earl of Godolphin, and grandson of Dorothy Berkeley, having married, in 1698, the Lady Henrietta Churchill, daughter of the great Earl, afterwards Duke, of Marlborough, and who herself became in her own right Duchess of Marlborough. On the occasion of this marriage, articles of settlement were entered into on 18th April, 1698; in pursuance of which a settlement was duly executed, on

PEDIGREE OF GODOLPHIN.

Margaret Killegrew = Sir Francis Godolphin, M.P. for Cornwall, *temp.* Elizabeth.
|
Sir William Godolphin = Thomasin Sidney.
M.P. for Cornwall, *temp.* James I.
|
Francis, = **DOROTHY BERKELEY**, of Yarlington.
cr. a knight at the coronation of Charles II.
|
SIR WILLIAM GODOLPHIN, created a baronet 1661, died 1710.
|
Sidney, = Margaret Blagge, m. 1675; d. Sept. 16, 1678.
Baron, 1684; Earl, 1706; K.G., Lord High Treasurer; d. 1712.
|
John, Earl of Marlboro'
|
Lady Henrietta Churchill, = **FRANCIS**, 2nd Earl Godolphin, m. 1698; d. 1766.
1702, Duchess of Marlboro' in her own right; succeeded to title 1722.
|
┌─────────────────────────────┬──────────────────────────────┐
HENRIETTA, = Sir Thomas Pelham,   **MARY**, = Thomas Osborne, Duke of Leeds, K.G., died 1789.
Duchess of Newcastle, cr. Duke of Newcastle 1715; died 1768. died 1776.   Duchess of Leeds, died 1764.
|
FRANCIS, Marquis of Carmarthen, born 1751; VENDOR, 1782.

20th July, 1723, of the Manor of Yarlington and other lands on the issue in tail of the Earl of Godolphin and Henrietta, then Duchess of Marlborough. They had two daughters co-heiresses, Henrietta and Mary, who married each a duke; Henrietta became Duchess of Newcastle, and Mary Duchess of Leeds. The Duchess of Newcastle suffered a recovery of her moiety in Hilary Term, 1769 (9 George III.), and dying without issue, by her will, proved in the Prerogative Court, 22nd July, 1776, devised her share to her nephew, Francis, Marquis of Carmarthen, who had, in Hilary Term, 1772 (12 George III.), suffered a recovery of the other half-share entailed upon his mother, the Duchess of Leeds, who had died some years before, in the life-time of her father, Francis, Earl of Godolphin. Lord Carmarthen thus became possessed of the entirety in fee.[1]

But to these great personages Yarlington was but as a drop in the ocean; probably they knew nothing of it beyond its name. After the death of Madam Jael Berkeley, in 1705, the Manor-house was allowed to dwindle into a farm-house, and is so described in a deed of 1723. There is, however, a small marble monument in the church to the memory of 'Mrs. Evelyn' (in the parish register entered as 'Susannah, wife of Charles Evelyn, esquire'), 'daughter

---

[1] As a specimen of the absolute worthlessness of Phelps' history, it may be as well to compare his statement with the above account. He says: 'Francis, Earl of Godolphin, who was Lord of the Manor in 1719, in pursuance of the articles made on his marriage with Henrietta, Duchess of Marlborough, in 1723, settled it in strict entail.' The marriage, in fact, took place in 1698; when the articles for a settlement were entered into. Phelps goes on to say: 'The Duchess of Newcastle, on her death, in 1772, left her moiety to her nephew, the Marquis of Carmarthen — the Marquis having likewise succeeded to his mother's moiety in 1782;' etc. Every date in the above statement is inaccurate, except the entirely irrelevant one that Francis, Earl of Godolphin, was Lord of the Manor in 1719—a position which, in fact, he held from 1710 to 1766.

of Peter Prideaux, esquire, of Solden, in Devonshire, wife of Charles Evelyn, esquire, who died 4th June, 1747, in the 39th year of her age.' The monument was erected by her husband; and the register records his own burial there on the 15th January, 1748, as that of 'Chas Evelyn, Esqre., son of Sir John Evelyn, of Surrey.' Their bodies were interred in a vault in the churchyard, which had necessarily to be disturbed on the occasion of the rebuilding and enlarging of the church by an additional aisle, in 1878. All that is known of them by tradition is, that the wife died whilst on a tour in which she passed through Yarlington. But as the Evelyns were closely connected, and on terms of intimate relationship with the Godolphins (John Evelyn of Wotton, in Surrey, being the well-known author of the life of Mrs. Sidney Godolphin, Dorothy Berkeley's daughter-in-law), it is only reasonable to suppose that the Evelyns were not chance travellers merely passing through the place, but that, in the course of their tour, they were spending a few days at the Godolphins' old Manor-house when Mrs. Evelyn was taken ill and died.

V.

THE MARQUIS OF CARMARTHEN.

VENDOR, 1782.

LORD CARMARTHEN himself, as a personage who at one time occupied a considerable space in public life, ought not to be passed over without notice. He was a man of varied accomplishments and of many talents, but 'high-falutin,' vain, and egotistical to the last degree. Born January, 1751, he married, in November, 1773, Amelia D'Arcy, only child of the Earl of Holdernesse, and in her own right Baroness Conyers, by whom he had two sons and one daughter. At the age of twenty-five he was, on his own pressing solicitations and those of his friends, called up to the House of Lords.[1] In the following year he applied for and obtained (December, 1777) the office of Lord Chamberlain to the Queen, and in July, 1778, was appointed Lord-Lieutenant of the East Riding of York. In May of this year 'poor Lord Holdernesse died.' And it is matter, perhaps, rather of regret than of surprise, that in the same year the fascinating and accomplished Lady Conyers, the idol of her father-in-law, the old Duke of Leeds, who was never so happy as when expatiating to his friends upon her merits

---

[1] The particulars in regard to Lord Carmarthen are mainly derived from the 'Political Memoranda of the Duke of Leeds,' edited by Oscar Browning, M.A., Camden Society, 1884.

and charms, wearied of the vanities and conceits of her somewhat feminine-natured lord, should have left him and her children to run off with plain Captain Jack Byron. The Marquis obtained a divorce in May, 1779; the lady married Captain Byron and had a daughter, afterwards the Honourable Augusta Leigh; and after the death (in 1784) of this, his first wife, Captain Jack Byron married Miss Gordon, and by her was father of Lord Byron, the poet.

In November of this year, 1779, in his character of Lord-Lieutenant of the East Riding, Lord Carmarthen made himself active in putting the coast and county on the defensive, against the attacks of Paul Jones; and the Marquis summoned his deputy-lieutenants and justices to a meeting at Beverley. In reference to this there is in Walpole's 'Letters' (vol. vii., p. 262) an amusing letter from his great friend and correspondent, Mason, written quite in Horace's own vein, and dated 'York, 12th November, 1779:'

'My Lord Carmarthen called upon me the other day on his return from the East Riding of this great county, where he had reviewed the whole coast, and found it so totally defenceless that he had given a ball at Beverley on the occasion. From York he retired to Kiveton, where, if he pleases, he may make another ball, and invite Lady Conyers to it, who, I don't doubt, will be pleased with such a fête; for you must know, at Lady Holdernesse's request, I have lent her my parsonage to reside in, while W. Byron is raising recruits at Sheffield and Rotherham.'

In his conduct of these affairs in Yorkshire, he found himself at variance with the Government, and consequently, on 27th January, 1780, he resigned the gold key of his office as Chamberlain; as Walpole himself writes, two days after: 'The *weathercock* Marquis has taken his part, or rather his leave, and resigned his key.' And on the 8th of February, the Marquis, with amusing particularity, notes in his diary: 'As I was going to dress, in order to attend the House of Lords, I received an official letter from the Secretary of State containing my dismissal from the offices of Lord-Lieutenant and Custos Rotulorum of the East Riding of Yorkshire. My surprise would scarcely have been greater had it been a warrant of commitment to the Tower.' He was appointed, in January, 1783, under Lord Shelburne's Administration, as Ambassador to France; but the break-up of the Ministry prevented the appointment from taking effect. However, upon Mr. Pitt's accepting the office of Prime Minister, in December, 1783, Lord Carmarthen received the seals of the Foreign Office, and held them until April, 1791, when he resigned, as not approving of concessions made by England to Russia as against the Turks, to which concessions our ally, Prussia, was also strongly opposed. He had succeeded to the dukedom in 1789. After resigning office he was perpetually scheming and planning—for it would be hardly fair to call it plotting or intriguing—to get a strong Government formed by Pitt and Fox both taking office; and his seven years' connection with Pitt gave him so little insight into the grandeur of that statesman's character, and his magnificent self-reliance, that he had actually brought himself to believe that such a coalition might be formed under himself as Prime Minister! Fox, indeed, was apparently not unwilling; but Pitt met his Grace's advances, first, with 'a very curt note,' and, finally, by declaring to him, at another interview, 'that there had been no thoughts of any alteration in the Government.'

The first Earl of Malmesbury, who was a personal friend of the Duke's, and was thrown into intimate relations with him at the Foreign Office, took good measure of his character and conduct on this occasion: 'The Duke of Leeds was in earnest, but, as he always is, carried away more by his imagination and sanguine hopes, *in which his string of toad-eaters encourage him*, than by reason and reflection ('Malmes. Diary,' vol. ii., p. 471).

These 'toad-eaters' pandered to his vanity, and of course looked up to him as their patron for promotion. Foremost amongst them was the Rev. Thomas Jackson—'my friend Jackson,' as he is termed over and over again by the Duke in his Diary, and for whom he is never weary of soliciting preferment. At the time of his sale of Yarlington, in 1782, to John Rogers, esquire, the ancestor of the present writer, there was a stipulation entered into, and a bond given to the vendor accordingly, that in case at the next vacancy of the living the purchaser should have no son of his own ready and willing to fill it, Mr. Jackson should have the preferment; Mr. Jackson, on his part, entering into a counter-bond to resign the preferment if, at any time after his presentation, any such son of the purchaser should wish to be appointed to the living.[1] At that time the living was held by a Mr. Gapper,

---

[1] This is not the first instance in the course of the narrative in which the right of presentation to the living has formed the subject of private or pecuniary arrangement; and the writer must plead guilty to being one of those simple-minded and old-fashioned moralists who fail to see anything worthy of blame in the transaction. On the contrary, the system appears to him to afford an opportunity for many a person to procure the presentation to the Bishop of a worthy friend or relative, who might otherwise be altogether passed over and be unnoticed. It opens the door to a larger number of fitly qualified candidates, from different grades of life—fitly qualified, be it said, for it must not be forgotten that the appointee must be, after all, a person who is already duly equipped for his work, and against whom no canonical objection can be taken.

one of a good old Somersetshire family. He died in the August of the same year. In the meantime Lord Carmarthen had obtained, in July, from Lord Shelburne, a prebendal stall in St. Paul's Cathedral for his friend; and on 6th September the Rev. Prebendary Jackson was duly inducted into the living of Yarlington. Early in the same year, in April, there had been a prospect of Lord Carmarthen's going to the Hague to negotiate terms of a treaty with Russia. He says: 'I had an application from the Bishop of Durham to let his son, Major Egerton, go with me as secretary, with which I complyed, and was assured the Bishop would be *happy to do something handsome for my friend Jackson*.'

In due course Mr. Prebendary Jackson (through the

A Bishop or lay-patron is not open to blame if he select for preferment a properly qualified friend or relation of his own; and the distinction is not very palpable where another purchases the right of presentation *pro hâc vice*, with a view to appointing such duly qualified friend or relation. As for any such purchaser being implicated in the sin of Simon Magus, there is really nothing whatever in common between his intentions and acts and those of Simon. The person who, *in order to get himself ordained*, finds himself under the obligation of feeing the official underlings of the Bishop, is brought much more closely within the mischief of Simon's offence. The writer is one of those who, far from thinking that 'establishment is a mere accident of the English Church,' believe, on the contrary, that establishment is of the essence of a National Church, that an Established Church and a National Church are in fact convertible terms; and further, and more especially, that it is precisely in the character of a National Church that the Anglican Church, as a branch Church, founds her strongest claims upon the allegiance of her people of this realm, as against the, perhaps, more imposing pretensions of the great Latin Church to be an Œcumenical or Universal Church, as distinguished from a National Church. Our zealous Church reformers of to-day may, doubtless, object that, in upholding these rights and privileges of patrons, the writer is in like case with Horace's friend Balbinus, who was enamoured of the polypus of his mistress, Agnes. It is not, however, to be supposed that the 'fair defects'—or the '*vitia ipsa*,' if you please—of the Establishment exercise any fascination over him; but he is strongly of opinion that the violent excision of these historic and venerable outgrowths would operate dangerously upon the vital interests of the Establishment itself, as the Church of the Nation.

influence of the Duke of Leeds when in Pitt's Cabinet) became Canon of St. Paul's, and Dr. Jackson. He had the character in the country of being a pompous, consequential sort of man, and it used to be said of him that whenever a vacancy occurred in the Episcopal Bench, he would get a paragraph inserted in the papers 'that it was generally expected that the lawn sleeves would be offered to Dr. Jackson.'

The Duke of Leeds was also much addicted to that most stupid of all pleasantries, the perpetration of practical jokes, and the following letter, written 17th January, 1810, by one of the Doctor's sons, George—afterwards Sir George—Jackson, to his mother, throws a curious light upon the relations subsisting between his Grace and his Grace's 'toad-eaters':

'I dined quite cozily and *en famille* at five o'clock with the Duchess of Leeds,[1] her sister, and a young man, a cousin of theirs, of the Anguish family. Her Grace seems to enjoy these little *parties fines*, where she can *jaser* at her ease of what evidently is a peculiar pleasure for her—bygone days.

'We had a little music, and afterwards, over a dish of tea, the Duchess told us some stories of the old Duke, whose fondness for practical jokes I have heard you speak of. She said that on one occasion, my father having arrived in London from Yarlington late in the evening and very tired, instead of going at once to Grosvenor Square, as he had proposed to do, went to his rooms in Davies Street, and to bed immediately. The Duke, being informed of this, ordered a cartload of straw to be laid down during the night under the windows of my father's room, and the knocker of the house-door to be tied up, to the great astonishment of the neighbours, and of my father's servant when he was called up next morning to answer the

---

[1] The Marquis of Carmarthen had remarried, in 1788, Catherine, daughter of Thomas Anguish, a Master in Chancery.

inquiries of an early message from his Grace respecting Dr. Jackson's health. Shortly after, other civil inquiries were made by two gentlemen who had been dining in Grosvenor Square, and by-and-by an invitation to dinner, in the doggerel rhyme in which the Duke and my father so often corresponded, was sent by the former. The Duchess could only recollect a few lines. They ran thus :

'" Dear Doctor,—To-day, if you're out of the hay,
  And to crawl to the Square should be able,
  At half after five you'll see how I thrive,
  With a Landgrave and Prince at my table."

' It went on to press him to " come and handle a ladle," which it appears he did, and that the joke served to make merry over at the table. I confess I think the Duke was rewarded for his trouble with but a small amount of fun.

' At another time, she said, Dr. Jackson having slipped away early from some entertainment to betake himself quietly to bed, was awakened from a sound nap by a dismal song, when, starting up in dismay, he beheld, surrounding his bed, a number of people wrapped in white sheets, carrying each a lighted candle and singing a doleful ditty, meant for a funeral dirge. It was the Duke and Duchess and other members of their family. Again, I must say I think the Duke's fun not worth so much trouble, literally " le jeu ne valait pas la chandelle." But the story made us laugh ; for the Duchess told it very well, and seemed so much amused at the recollection, as she said, of the Doctor's bewilderment on awaking, and his jovial laugh when he found that, instead of being in the lower regions, as he declared their unearthly howlings made him suppose, he was surrounded only by a party of mirth-loving friends.

'G. J.'

Such was the *desipientia*, out of place and unseemly, with which this accomplished but rather feather-brained statesman beguiled his leisure hours. In the latter part of his life he was beginning to take an interest in the fortunes of that most uninteresting personage, Caroline, Princess of Wales. Dr. Jackson died 1st December, 1797, and his ducal friend and patron 31st January, 1799. But although Dr. Jackson may have been disappointed in the matter of the lawn sleeves, yet his patron did him a much greater service by making use of his influence at the Foreign Office to get the Doctor's eldest son, Francis, into the diplomatic service, which was afterwards followed by the next, and much younger, son, George (the writer of the foregoing letter), being also engaged in the same department; where they both filled most important positions on the Continent, being employed at the European Courts during the eventful period of, and after, the Napoleonic wars.

Their letters, principally to their mother, and their Diaries, are comprised in four volumes, two called 'The Diaries and Letters of Sir George Jackson,' and two called 'The Bath Archives,' published in 1873 by Lady Jackson (Sir George Jackson's widow), and are full of interest. It is abundantly evident that their mother, Mrs. Charlotte Jackson, who moved from Yarlington to Bath after Dr. Jackson's death, and who had to look after a family of sons and daughters, was quite one of ten thousand, and was held in much respect and devotion by her two prosperous sons. Her letters in these volumes seem worthy to rank with the very best specimens of letter-writing that have been handed down to us. The following, written to her son George on the 10th January, 1810, and which was answered in the week after by his letter just quoted, may serve as an example :

'10*th*.

'It is strange that so few letters are received from Francis,[1] and that he omits writing by the regular packets. I always make allowance for more important avocations, but it would never enter into my head that I was forgotten, so that your consoling suggestion, my dear George, was not needed. To forget my children, or to be forgotten by them, will be a sensation I humbly trust I shall never be sensible of. Of all misfortunes, that, I think, would be the worst.

'From having other thoughts in my mind, I have let pass two letters without answering your question of whether Dr. Johnson did not die in the same year in which you were born. I know not how you could get that fancy into your head. Dr. Johnson died in 1784, and, I believe, in December. I remember we used sometimes to meet him and Mrs. Piozzi at our friends' houses. Your father thought much of him, and used generally to say, "The Doctor talked grandly to-night," or "growled Mr. Such-an-one into silence." How young men could admire him I could not understand, but I must own he was no favourite of mine. He was very learned, I have no doubt, and his Lexicon proved that he knew the meaning of most things; yet, with all that, he never seemed to be able to comprehend what good manners meant. He was pompous and overbearing, and unpardonably untidy—faults I remarked in other clever men of his day. But, for my part, I could never see in genius and learning an excuse for a deliberate breach of decorum, such as appearing amongst less gifted folks in snuffy shirt-frills and soiled vestments; or consider rudeness of speech and rough manners the marks of a superior mind.

'How Mrs. Piozzi could only tolerate so coarse and bear-like a person as the Doctor used to surprise me, and much more how she could conduct herself with the levity she did. Their manners were more disgusting than pleasing to most persons, and I was not alone in my opinion that they both ought to have been ashamed of themselves.

'I shall think *you* ought to be ashamed of yourself if you don't tell me more regularly what is going on. As you have no despatches to write—

---

[1] Mr. F. Jackson was at this time in America, engaged in a difficult and delicate negotiation with the United States, which, however, proved unsuccessful.

though you seem to have taken up your quarters at the Foreign Office, and write all your letters there, as your father did when the Duke of Leeds held office—you may at least tell me of the *trifles* that are going on around you; for the conviction that you will seize your pen to inform me without delay of *anything important* that may occur does not satisfy me.

'C. J.'

But we seem to have travelled far away from Yarlington. Let us hasten home before the curtains are closed and the night has set in.

It has been mentioned that Yarlington had been visited by perhaps the most vicious of all our kings—King John; and the narrative comes to an end with a little anecdote in connection with one of the most virtuous of our monarchs.

Upon completion of the purchase in 1782, the grandfather of the present writer, having inspected the 'old Berkeley Mansion,' as it was then called, pronounced it 'picturesque, but damp,' and somewhat ruthlessly let off the water of the lake, which had now assumed the character of a succession of large fish-ponds,[1] and did away with Fitz-James's Mill, bringing away much of the materials of the old Manor-house to the place where he had decided to build without delay a new mansion. The site was a treeless plain, or common, of forty or fifty acres, on a high plateau, open to every blast, and quite unsheltered from the northwest winds, which are most prevalent here.

The late Mr. Hobhouse (grandfather of our present M.P.) has told me, that in his boyhood it was 'the most destitute,

---

[1] In 1687 a lease for seven years is granted by Sir William Godolphin, Jael Berkeley, and Harry Roynon, of West Harptree, esquire, of Yarlington Farm, *except the mansion-house, fish-ponds and gardens.*

desolate place he ever beheld.' At the time the house was building, George III. passed along the main road in front of it, on his way from Weymouth to Longleat, on a visit to Lord Weymouth; and my grandfather, who was then living at South Cadbury Rectory while the house was in course of erection, came up with his family to the turnpike road at Yarlington, which runs in front of it, to salute his Majesty as he passed by. Seeing the building going on, the King asked who was doing that. On being informed that it was the work of a new Squire who had recently purchased the Manor, his Majesty observed in his peculiar style, 'Hah! hah! a bold man, a bold man, to build a house there.'

Corrigendum.

IT is mentioned—*ante*, p. 8—as on the authority of Mr. Dickinson, of Kingweston, that two persons of the name of 'Gyon,' or 'Gyan,' were entered as living at Yarlington at the Inquisition held before the Lord Treasurer, John de Kerkbye, and reference was made to Mr. Dickinson's promised publication of that 'Quest.'

After the foregoing pages had been well advanced in the press, this valuable contribution to the 'Somerset Records' duly appeared, when I discovered that those names were entered—not in Kirkby's or Kirby's Quest, but—at p. 101, in the 'Tax Roll of 1 Edward III.,' which, under the heading of 'Exchequer Lay Subsidies,' is included, together with other documents in the volume, under the general title of 'Kirby's Quest.' The mistake in confusing the two lists or subjects is entirely my own, and I therefore not unnaturally make haste to withdraw my hand from the apprehended ferule of my good friend, Mr. Dickinson. In fact, 'the Lord John de Kerkbye,' the Treasurer, is stated in the Preface, at p. xviii., to have died in 1290, 18 Edward I.

Further, in reference to the suggestion hazarded—*ante*, p. 8—that Domesday may have included Woolston in the adjoining parish of Blackford, it is observable that in the 'Nomina Villarum' of Edward II., Hamo Fitz-Richard, who is returned as part-lord of Blackford, is also entered as Lord of the hamlet of Woolston ('Kirby's Quest,' pp. 53-59). And we learn from Collinson, iii. 452, that, at an Inquisition held 35 Edward III., a portion of Blackford was found to be held of the Earl of Salisbury at a rent service of 3s. 4d. The Bamfyldes, who inherited portions of Blackford, seem to form a connecting link with Bamfield Chafin, referred to in the note to p. 9, *ante*. I should add that the modern acreage of Blackford is, by a misprint, stated to be 578, and is 703 acres.

APPENDIX.

LIST OF INCUMBENTS.

SEPULCHRALIA.

LIST OF INCUMBENTS.

DATE OF INSTITUTION	INCUMBENT.	PATRON.
1314	William de Glideford	
1321	John de Crokes Eston	Rex, as guardian of William, son of Wm. de Montacute.
1323	Matthew Husee	,, ,,
,,	William Pencrich	,, ,,
1340	Jas. Sonford de Stanlake	Wm. de Montacute, Com. Sarum.
1342	Thomas Threske	Wm. de Montacute, Com. Sarum.
	(Robertus Saunders)	
	Robert Colbwude	
1418, September 5	Richard Bailly *al.* Chamberlayne.	John Bailly and others.
1452, February 2	Thos. Chauntre, A.M.	Ric. Comes Sarum.
1456, March 13	Alex Cressingham	Ric. Comes Sarum.
1462, April 3	Edward Massy	Alicia, Comitissa Sarum.
1463, January 31	Thos. Chauntre, A.M.	Ric. Com. Warwick et dom. Sarum.
	John Newman	
1493, March 22	Thos. Hobbys, A.M.	Henry VII. Rex.
1497, March 5	John Steryge	Henry VII., Rex.
	William Nicholson	

DATE OF INSTITUTION.	INCUMBENT.	PATRON.
1555, May 22	Roger Boydell	Thomas Smyth, mil.
1573, April 11	William Rosewell	Thos. Rosewell de Dunkerton and another, by concession of Wm. Rosewell de Loxton, gent.
1627, February 1	William Clifford, A.M.	John Thatcher.
1634, November 27	Bernard Bangor,[1] A.M.	Bamfield Chafin, arm.
1673, September 25	John Randall, A.B.	Maurice Berkeley, arm.
1679, August 2	Joseph Barker, A.M.	Katherine Barker, widow, on the grant of Jael Berkeley.
1723, July 25	Edward Cozens, A.B.	Fran. Comes Godolphin.
1754, January 1	Richard Gapper, B.A.	Fran. Comes Godolphin.
1765, October 1	Richard Gapper,[2] B.A.	Fran. Comes Godolphin.
1782, September 5	Thomas Jackson, M.A.	John Rogers, esquire.
1797, December 23	Roger Frankland, M.A.	John Rogers, esquire.

[1] It is interesting to note that whatever may have been the circumstances under which Bamfield Chafin, esquire, obtained this presentation from Sir Henry Berkeley, the presentee, Bernard Bangor, was one of those who have the honour of being named in Walker as having been ejected from his living by Parliament. The entry by Walker is significant, as suggestive of the confusion and duplicity prevailing under the oppression of the Puritans. The extract is as follows (part ii., p. 207):

'BANGOR, YARLINGTON R.

'He had at that time a wife and family. His successor was one Dorington, a reputed papist; who (as himself afterwards confessed to the gentleman who informed me of this) was bred at St. Omers, and designed for physick. Mr. B. survived the usurpation, and therefore, in all probability, returned to his living.'

Bangor was, in fact, restored in 1660, and enjoyed the living for thirteen years afterwards.

[2] It appears that for some reason this Richard Gapper must have resigned the living, and have been re-instituted to it on 1st October, 1765, as he is mentioned in the Diocesan Register to have been presented by Francis. Earl of Godolphin, on the cession *of him, the said Richard Gapper.*

DATE OF INSTITUTION.	INCUMBENT.	PATRON.
1826, May 18	... Robert Green Rogers, M.A.	... Anne Reynolds Rogers, widow.
1876, June 3	... Arthur Johnson Rogers, M.A.	... The Rev. Arthur Johnson Rogers.

All the foregoing entries, down to and including the presentation of Edward Cozens, A.B., in 1723, are taken from 'Somerset Incumbents,' a work quite recently and most carefully edited by the Rev. F. W. Weaver, M.A., of the Vicarage, Milton Clevedon, Bruton.

SEPULCHRALIA.

SEPULCHRALIA.

IN THE CHURCH.

NORTH SIDE OF CHANCEL.

Two Brasses.

1.

To the Glory of God
and in memory of
the Rev. ROBERT G. ROGERS, M.A.
Born 6th November, 1800.   Died 19th March, 1876
He was Rector of this Parish
for fifty years.
'There remaineth a rest for the people of God

2.

Here lie the bodies of
MARY THEODORA, 1st wife of the Rev. R. G. Rogers, A.M.,
Rector of this Parish,
the eldest daughter of the Rev. John Johnson, Ll.D.,
Rector of Yaxham-with-Welborne, Norfolk,
who died May 6th, 1836.   Aged 26 years.
Also of LUCY JUDITH, his 2nd wife,
2nd daughter of the Rev. Charles Pine-Coffin, A.M.,
Rector of East Downe, Devonshire,
who died August 30th, 1846.   Aged 35 years.
Also of EMILY GERTRUDE, her 2nd daughter,
who died January 19th, 1846.   Aged 18 months.
'We look for the resurrection of the dead, and the life
of the world to come.'

IN THE TOWER TRANSEPT.

West Wall.

A Large Monument of Black Marble set in Bath Stone.

In a Vault
on the North side of the Chancel
are deposited the Remains of
JOHN ROGERS, Esquire,
Lord of this Manor,
who died February xxviii, MDCCCXXI,
in the lxxviiith year of his age.
Also those of
ANN REYNOLDS, his wife,
who died April xxiv, MDCCCXLVI,
in the xciind year of her age.
He was the only Son
of Thomas Rogers, Esqre., of Besford Court,
and of the Parish of All Saints', Worcester,
and was Sheriff of this County
in the year MDCCCIV.
She was the only Child
of Pickering Robinson, Esqre.,
of Rawcliffe, in the County of York.

' Yet a little while and He that shall come will come, and will not tarry.'—Heb. x. 37.

Arms : Argent, 3 stags trippant sa. attired or,
a chief azure (Rogers),
on an escutcheon of pretence,
Vert, a chevron between 3 bucks trippant or
(Robinson).

IN THE TOWER TRANSEPT.

East Wall.

Brass.

In dutiful remembrance
Of FRANCIS ROGERS, Esquire, Lord of this Manor
and Representative of a Family of that Name
which in the Sixteenth Century held a leading place
amongst the Citizens of Bristol, and was afterwards
of Eastwood Park, Gloucestershire.
He died April 5th, 1863, in the 79th year of his Age.
Also in Memory of CATHERINE ELIZABETH,
Widow of the above-named Francis Rogers,
and eldest daughter of Benjamin Bickley, Esqre.,
of Bristol, and of Ettingshall Lodge, Staffordshire.
She died February 14th, 1881, Aged 89 years and four months,
and is buried with her Husband
In the Family Vault.

IN THE NAVE.

Oval Marble Monument.

M. S.
of
FREDERICK JOHN WILLIAM,
Son of the Rev. Thos. Jackson, D.D.,
Rector of this Parish,
and Charlotte, his wife,
who died an Infant Nov. 23rd, 1790.
Also of
MARIANNE, their daughter,
who died August 30th, 1791,
in the 19th year of her age.
She fell by an early, not premature death.
For the eminent virtues she displayed,
which endeared her to her family
and procured her universal esteem,
with her exemplary resignation
to the will of Heaven,
fitted her
for the participation of its bliss.

IN THE NORTH AISLE.

Two Marble Monuments.

1.

Near this place
lies Interred
MRS. EVELYN,
Daughter of
Peter Prideaux, Esqr.,
of Solden, in Devonshire,
Wife of
Charles Evelyn, Esqr.,
who died June iv,
MDCCXLVII,
In the xxxix year of her Age.

2.

Near this place
Are Deposited the Remains of
MRS. ANNE BURCHALL,
who departed this life the
15th of December, 1834,
Aged 90 years.

'Though lost to sight,
To memory dear.'

IN THE CHURCHYARD.

Flat Stone (moved from the Chancel in 1877).

Here lie the Remains of the
REV. RICHARD GAPPER, A.B., late Rector of
this Parish, who departed this life, Aug. 10,
A.D. 1782, aged 65.
A worthy Parish Priest and sincere honest Man.
Likewise the body of Mrs. MARY GAPPER, late of
Shaston, Dorset, his Venerable Mother, who died
May, 1770, aged —.
Also
Here are deposited the remains of
ISABELLA GAPPER, widow and relict of the above-named
Richard Gapper. She departed this life June,
1784, aged —.

Arms : Gules, a saltire, in chief, 3 lions rampant.

Flat Stone (moved from the Nave of Church in 1877).

Here lyeth the
Body of THOMAS The
Sonne of Thomas Brooke
And Elinor His Wife
Gent, Who Died The Fifth
Day of June Anno 17—.

All Flesh Is Grass The Life Of Man
A Shadow Or At Best A Span
Our Wit Our Learning Or Our Art
Are Vain When Death Presents His Dart.

Head-Stones.

To RICHARD SYMS, who died
Octr. ye 19th, 1745,
Aged 82.
Also to MARY his wife, who died
Octr. ye 16th, 1743.

In Memory of
WILLIAM SYMS,
d. Nov. 24, 1871, aged 68.
Also of
JANE, his beloved wife,
d. Sep. 29, 1869, aged 68.

In Memory
of
LEVI GARLAND,
During 45 years.
Clerk of this Parish.

"Well done, thou good
and faithful servant."

In Memory of
RICHARD DAVIDGE,
For 29 years clerk of
Yarlington Church,
Who died Apl. 5, 1868,
aged 61.

"Yet will I rejoice in the Lord;
I will joy in the God of my salvation."

In Memory of
SAMUEL EASTMENT,
who died Feby. 27th,
1779, aged 31 years.

Death in my prime gave me a fall
Who took me from my Wife and Children small;
Grieve not for me, my Glass is run :
It is God's Will, and must be done.

Here lies the Body of MARTHA,
Wife of John Chalmers, who died
June 12th, 1798, aged 62 years.

Also
of JOHN CHALMERS, late Gardener
of Yarlington Lodge,
and under the same Master
for upwards of thirty-seven years.
He died June 19th, 1812, aged 77 years.

If simple Truth in rustic manners drest,
If Worth in humble garb may claim its own,
Then Reverence the Earth where Virtue rests,
And leave to worthless Pride its poor renown.

In Memory of
JAMES HILL, of this Parish,
who died Dec. 29, 1868,
Aged 80 years.
He passed the greater part
of his life in the household
of Francis Rogers, Esquire,
the trusty servant of a
grateful master.

Also of ANN,
wife of the above-named James Hill,
who died Feby. 2, 1865,
aged 75 years.

Head-Stones (Marble).

In
Affectionate Remembrance of
ROSE ANNA,
wife of
Daniel Arthur,
who died March 3rd, 1871,
in her 53rd year.
" Thy Will be done."

Also of the above
DANIEL ARTHUR,
who died Jany. 27th, 1881,
aged 68 years.
"We all do fade as a leaf."

(*Stone.*)

To JOAN PENNY, d. June 30, 1782, aged 63.
To FRANCIS PENNY, d. July 21, 1827, aged 73;
and to MARTHA his wife, d. Feb. 23, 1833, aged 79.
(With original verse.)

Also to WILLIAM, son of Francis and Martha
Penny, who died Nov. 2, 1798, aged 21 years.

Like as a Dart Death struck my heart
While in my youthful prime ;
My Friends most dear, your grief forbear ,
Trust God's appointed time.

Sacred to the Memory
of JOHN BIDDISCOMBE,
who died May 1, 1833, aged 52 years.

Also of MARY, his wife,
who died Dec. 1, 1840, aged 63 years.
(Two verses : ' A sufferer in this vale of tears,' etc.)

Here lyeth the Body of
RICHARD CORNISH, who dy'd Dec. 7th, 1747, aged 42.
Also ANN, daughter of Richard and
Barbara Cornish, who dy'd Jan. 28, 1759, aged 19 ;
MARY, another of their daughters, who died
Sept., 1782, aged 49 years.

Young men and maids serve God betime,
For Death took me just in my prime ;
So may it you, therefore I pray
Make use of your time now while you may.

Altar Tombs.

In Memory of RICHARD SYMS, d. Jan. 30, 1781, aged 63.
Also of JOSEPH SYMS, ob. June 4, 1781, aged 68.

Thy Goodness and thy tender Care
Have all his hopes outdone ;
A Crown of Gold thou mad'st him wear,
And sett'dst it firmly on.
He prayd for Life, and Thou, O Lord,
Didst to his prayer attend,
And graciously to him afford
Life that shall never end.

Ps. xxi. *v*. 3 & 4.

To JOHN CORNISH,
who died 11th March, 1740,
aged 37.
And ANN his wife.

Also in Memory of ROBERT, their son, who died
at St. John's College, Cambridge, and
Interred there 8th June, 1749, aged 20;
and of JOHN, their son, who died 19th May,
1755, aged 28;
and of RICHARD, their son, who died 24th Sept.,
1766, aged 33 years.

Crosses (Marble).

Sacred to the Memory
of
NORA EWING ROGERS,
wife of the Rector of this Parish.
She died 24th May, 1878,
aged 20 years.
" In Thy presence is the fulness of joy;
at Thy right hand are there pleasures
for evermore."

(*Free-Stone.*)

In Memory
of JAMES WHITE, who died Apl. 16, 1873, aged 69,
of MARY, his wife, who died Aug. 28, 1865, aged 67,
and of ALFRED WHITE, who d. July 7, 1880, aged 40.

NOTE.—The list of head-stones is not exhaustive. Those have been for the most part selected which record the names of families connected with the parish for many generations.

INDEX.

Bangor, Rev. Bernard, ejected and restored, 78
Barker, Rev. Joseph, 53, 54
Bayntun, Henry, of Stavordale and Roundhill, 34, 48
Berkeley, Sir Henry, of Bruton: his will, 29
„ Sir Henry, of Yarlington, 31 *et seq.*
„ Madam Jael, 45 *et seq.*
„ Dame Margaret: her will, 35
„ Maurice, of Yarlington, 42
„ of Stratton, Lord: his will, 33

Carmarthen, Marquis of, 61 *et seq.*
Chafin, Family of, 9
Chaucer, Alice, 13
Clothier, William: his services (?), 59
Coke, Sir Edward: his style, 38
Cottington, Francis, Lord, 36

Davis, John, of Wells, 57
Deer's Leap, The, 6, 9
Donyatt, 4
Drokensford's Register, 3

Earth, Joseph, 31, 37
„ Roger, 37
Elizabeth, Princess, 23
Evelyn, Mr. and Mrs. Charles, 61, 62
Eyton's Domesday, 2

Fitz-James: his mill, 26, 72

Galhampton, 30
George III., King, 73
Godolphin, Sir W., 47, 55
„ Sidney, 59
Gyon or Guihane, 9

Hobhouse, Right Hon. Hy., 11, 72

Huntingdon, Earl of, releases rent-charge, 34

Jackson, Rev. Thomas, 66 *et seq.*
„ Francis and George, 70
John, King, 5
Johnson, Dr., Mrs. Jackson on, 71
Jones, Sir William: his opinion, 48, 52

Killegrews, The, 32
'King-maker,' The, 13

Lewis, Peter Roynon, 58

Mary, Queen, 23, 24
Maynard, Serjt., 46
Mildmay, Mr.: his loan, 43, 50, 55
Montacute, 3
Montacute, Simon de, 3, 5, 17
Mortain, Earl of, 2

Neville, Sir H., of Billingsbere, 32
Norwood Park, 28, 29

Parr, Queen Katharine, 20, 22
Parr, Wm., Marquis of Northampton, 21

Rosewell, Family of, 25, 27
Roynon, Peter, 40, 47, 56
„ Harry, 55, 57, 58

Salisbury, Margaret, Countess of, 16
Shandy, Mr. Walter: his theory, 45
Shepton Montague (*caput baroniæ*), 4
Smalldon, 34, 41, 47, 51
Smith, Sir Thomas, 21
Southworths, The, 35, 37

Warwick, Edward Plantagenet, Earl of, 14
Woolston Farm, 8, 9, 74

Yarlington Fair, 20, 40

THE END.

Elliot Stock, Paternoster Row, London.

www.ingramcontent.com/pod-product-compliance
Lightning Source LLC
Chambersburg PA
CBHW021946160426
43195CB00011B/1247